WREXHAM
TO
NEW BRIGHTON

Vic Mitchell and Keith Smith

MP Middleton Press

Published August 2013

ISBN 978 1 908174 47 5

© Middleton Press, 2013

Design Deborah Esher
Typesetting Barbara Mitchell

Published by
      Middleton Press
      Easebourne Lane
      Midhurst
      West Sussex
      GU29 9AZ
Tel: 01730 813169
Fax: 01730 812601
Email: info@middletonpress.co.uk
www.middletonpress.co.uk

Printed in the United Kingdom by Henry Ling Limited, at the Dorset Press, Dorchester, DT1 1HD

ACKNOWLEDGEMENTS

We are very grateful for the assistance received from many of those mentioned in the credits, also to A.R.Carder, A.J.Castledine, G.Croughton, M.Dart, R.Geach, S.C.Jenkins, P.Kelly, N.Langridge, Mr D. and Dr S.Salter, M.Turvey and in particular, our always supportive wives, Barbara Mitchell and Janet Smith.

INDEX

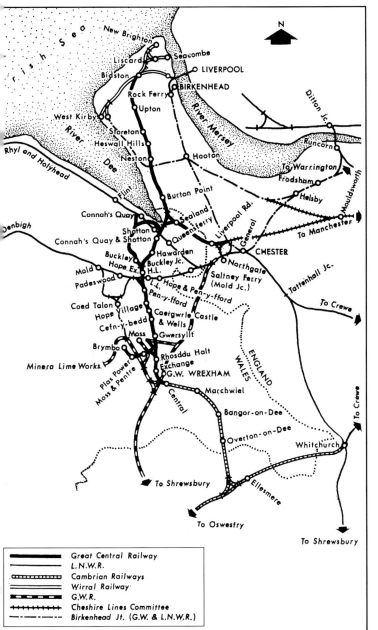

I. Pre-1923 route operators and the national boundary are shown. Welsh spellings are discussed in the captions. (Railway Magazine)

GEOGRAPHICAL SETTING

Regarded by many as the commercial capital of North Wales, Wrexham is only five miles from England. Our route is fairly level for three miles and it then descends into the valley of the River Alyn, along which it takes an undulating course.

The line north to the Dee Estuary was built near the border of Flintshire and Denbighshire and it traversed a productive coalfield. The area also provided much clay for pipe and brick making. Tramways were laid exclusively for this traffic in the Buckley-Connah's Quay area, these being replaced by railway branches.

The route passes over the River Dee on Hawarden Bridge and enters the largely flat landscape of Cheshire.

The peninsula is known as The Wirral and the line to Chester ran across its southern border. Our journey ends near the dockland of Birkenhead, having crossed mainly sandstone.

The maps are to the scale of 25ins to 1 mile, with north at the top unless otherwise indicated. Furthermore as Welsh spelling and hyphenation has varied over the years, we have generally used the form of the period.

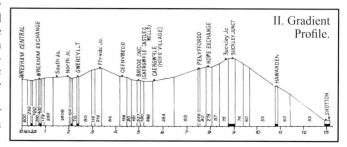

II. Gradient Profile.

HISTORICAL BACKGROUND

An outline of the network development in the area is necessary before looking at details of the route. The Crewe-Chester and the Birkenhead-Chester sections opened on different dates in 1840.

The Shrewsbury & Chester Railway was completed north of Ruabon in 1846, although the northern two miles belonged to the Chester & Holyhead Railway. This opened west to Bangor in 1848 and the Buckley Railway constructed a branch south from it at Connah's Quay. This opened for freight in 1862.

The Wrexham, Mold & Connah's Quay Railway opened on 1st May 1866, carrying passengers between Buckley and Wrexham from then until 31st March 1890. The original Buckley station reopened from 1893 to 1895. The company opened north from Buckley Junction to Chester Northgate on 31st March 1890, plus a freight branch from Shotton to Connah's Quay. At Wrexham, the company extended services from Exchange to Central stations on 1st November 1887. The latter station was reached by trains of Cambrian Railways from Ellesmere from 2nd November 1895. This company became part of the Great Western Railway in 1922. The line was in use until 1940 and again from 1946 to 1965, for passengers.

Chester Northgate had been opened by the Cheshire Lines Committee on 1st May 1875 to receive trains from Manchester. The route westwards to Dee Junction was the property of the Manchester, Sheffield & Lincolnshire Railway, which became part of the Great Central Railway in 1897. The North Wales & Liverpool Railway opened northwards from Dee Junction to Bidston on 18th March 1896 and this became a GCR constituent in 1906. The Buckley Railway and the WM&CQR had been incorporated therein in 1905.

The line through Bidston was opened by the Hoylake Railway on 2nd July 1866 and it carried passengers between Hoylake and Birkenhead. The line then became part of the Hoylake & Birkenhead Rail & Tramway.

The route north of Bidston was opened to New Brighton by the Seacombe, Hoylake & Deeside Railway on 30th August 1888 and the branch from it to Seacombe followed in 1895. The routes north, east and west of Bidston, together with the Seacombe branch, became the Wirral Railway in 1891 and part of the London Midland & Scottish Railway in 1923. At this time, the GCR became a constituent of the London & North Eastern Railway.

The LMS electrified the New Brighton route in 1938, using conductor rails at 650 volts DC. They were later increased to 750 volts. Upon nationalisation in 1948, the LMS became the London Midland Region of British Railways, while most of the LNER formed the Eastern. (Scotland excepted in both cases.) The GWR became the Western Region. The routes in this album were allocated to the LMR, however. The Seacombe branch closed to passengers on 4th January 1960 and totally on 17th June 1963.

After privatisation, the line was operated by North Western Trains south of Bidston from 2nd March 1997. North, east and west thereof, the franchisee was Merseyrail from 19th January 1997. The franchise for the Wrexham-Bidston service was held by Arriva Trains Wales from 1st August 2003, while north of Bidston, it was Merseyrail Electrics from 19th January 1997 until 17th February 2000, when Arriva Trains Merseyrail took over. From 23rd April 2003 Abelio/Serco ran trains as Merseyrail.

PASSENGER SERVICES

From Wrexham

The initial service to Buckley comprised three return trips, weekdays only. Sunday figures are shown in brackets hereon and only trains running at least four days per week are mentioned. By 1878 the figure was 5 (0) and by 1887 it was 6 (0).

Extension to Chester in 1890 brought 5 (0) trains, with 4 (1) more terminating at Buckley. Opening of the line to Seacombe in 1895 resulted in 12 (5) trains from the south terminating there. However, 5 (3) started at Chester Northgate, instead of Wrexham.

Similar ratios were maintained and by 1948, the Seacombe terminations numbered 9 (3) and Chester received 5 (1). There were also a few short workings between Hawarden and Chester. After the Seacombe branch closed in 1960, all trains were diverted to New Brighton. Almost hourly, trains from Wrexham were terminated at Birkenhead North from January 1971. They all reversed at Bidston from October 1978, reducing congestion on the busy electrified lines.

To New Brighton

The initial timetable showed an hourly service, but with no trains on Sunday mornings. The 1958 electric pattern had trains every 10 minutes at peak times, 20 minutes off-peak and 30 minutes on Sundays. By 2013, the figures were 15 daytime and 30 evenings and Sundays.

June 1869

November 1894

WREXHAM, HOPE, CONNAH'S QUAY, CHESTER, BIDSTON, BIRKENHEAD, SEACOMBE, and LIVERPOOL.

North Wales and Liverpool and Wrexham, Mold, and Connah's Quay.

Down.	Fares from Wrexham: Single 1 cl.	Single 3 cl.	Return 1 cl.	Return 3 cl.	mrn	mrn	mrn	mrn	mrn	mrn	mrn	aft	mrn	aft	aft
347 Aberystwyth ...dep.													8 50		
Oswestry 347 ... ״										8 40			1140		
Ellesmere 348 .. ״										9 5			12 5		
Wrexham (Central ..dep.						6 55	7 55		9 8	10 0			1255	2 15	
״ (Exchange) ...							7 58		9 11	10 3			1258	2 18	
Gwersyllt						7 2	8 2		9 15	10 7			1 2	2 22	
Cefn-y-bedd						7 7	8 7		9 20	1012			1 7	2 27	
Bridge End						7 9	8 9			1014			1 9	2 29	
Caergwrle						7 12	8 13			1016				2 31	
Pen-y-ffordd						7 17	8 18		9 27	1021			1 15	2 36	
Hope (Exchange) 357						7 29	8 20		9 29	1023			1 17	2 38	
Buckley Junction						7 32	8 23		9 32	1026			1 20	2 41	
Hawarden							8 30		9 38	1033			1 27	2 48	
Connah's Quay * ... arr.							8 35		9 43	1038			1 32	2 53	
Connah's Quay * ..dep.							8 42			1045			1 37	3 5	
Saughall							8 49			1052			1 44	3 12	
Blacon							8 54			1057			1 49	3 17	
Chester (L'pool Rd.).ar.							8 57			11 0			1 52	3 20	
״ (Northgate) ״							9 0			11 3			1 55	3 23	
Chester (Northgate).dp.							8 15	8 40		1015	1135		1 10	2 30	3 10
״ (Liverpool Rd.)							8 17	8 42		1017	1137		1 12	2 32	3 12
Blacon							8 20			1020	1140		1 15	2 35	
Saughall							8 25	8 48		1025	1145		1 20	2 40	3 18
Connah's Quay * ..arr.							8 33			1033			1 28	2 48	
Connah's Quay * ....dep.							8 36		9 44	1039			1 33	2 54	
Neston and Parkgate					8 18		8 47	8 59	9 55	1050	1156	1230	1 44	3 5	3 29
Heswall Hills					8 24		8 53	9 5	10 1	1056	12 2	1236	1 50	3 11	3 35
Storeton					8 29		Sig.		10 6	11 1	12 7				Sig.
Upton					8 34		9 1	9 13	1011	11 6	1212	1244	1 58	3 19	3 43
Bidston 352					8 39		9 6	9 18	1016	1111	1217	1249	2 4	3 24	3 48
Birkenhead Docks									11 3	12 1	1 1	1 1	3 1		4 8
Birkenhead Park					8 54				11 6	12 4	1 4	1 4	3 4		4 11
״ (Hamilton Sq.)									1112	1211	1 11	1 11	3 11		4 22
L'pool (James St.).arr.					9 2				1116	1215	1 15	1 15	3 15		4 26
״ (Cen., L. L.) ״					9 4				1118	1217	1 17	1 17	3 17		4 29
Liscard and Poulton 352							9 9		1019	1114					
Seacombe ....arr.					8 45		9 13	9 24	1023	1118	1223	1255	2 10	3 30	3 54
Liverpool (Lan. Stage) ״					8 56		9 26	9 36	1036	1136	1236	1 6	2 21	3 51	4 6

Down.	aft	aft	aft	aft	aft	aft	aft	aft	aft	aft	aft	Sundays: mrn	mrn	aft	aft	aft
347 Aberystwyth ...dep.		12 5								2 15						
Oswestry 347 ... ״		2 55								5 32						
Ellesmere 348 .. ״		3 15							7 15	7 15						
Wrexham (Central ..dep.		3 45		5 30				a Stops on Mondays and Saturdays.	7 45	8 40	9 30	8 25			5 45	
״ (Exchange) ...		3 48		5 33						8 43						
Gwersyllt				5 37					7 52	8 47	9 37	8 32			5 52	
Cefn-y-bedd				5 42					7 59	8 52	9 43	8 37			5 57	
Bridge End	3b27			5 44			7 50		8 0	8 54	9 46	8 39			5 59	
Caergwrle				5 46							9 49	8 41			6 1	
Pen-y-ffordd				5 51						8 59	9 55	8 46			6 6	
Hope (Exchange) 357	3b35			5 53			7 58			0 1						
Buckley Junction	3b38			5 56			8 1			9 3	9 59	8 50			6 10	
Hawarden	3 45			6 3	6 10		8 8			9 10	10 6	8 57			6 17	
Connah's Quay * ... arr.	3 50			6 8	6 15		8 13			9 15	1011	9 2			6 22	
Connah's Quay * ..dep.	Mons., Thurs., and Sats.				6 16		Mons., Thurs., and Sats.		Saturdays only.	9 55	1012					
Saughall					6 23					10 2						
Blacon					6 28					10 7						
Chester (L'pool Rd.).ar.		4 29			6 31					1010	1025					
״ (Northgate) ״					6 34					1013	1028					
Chester (Northgate).dp.		Thro' Carriage to Manchester (Cen.) arriving at 5 30 aft. See page 523.	5 40					8 35			Saturdays only.		10 5	5 5		8 1
״ (Liverpool Rd.)			5 42					0 07					10 7	5 7		8 1
Blacon			5 45										1010	5 10		8 2
Saughall			5 50					8 43					1015	5 15		8 2
Connah's Quay * ..arr.																
Connah's Quay * ....dep.	3 51			6 9			8 14			9 16		9 3			6 23	
Neston and Parkgate	4 2		6 1	6 22		6 40	8 25	8 54		9 27		9 14	1026	5 26	6 34	8 3
Heswall Hills	4 8		6 7	6 28		6 46	8 31	9 0		9 33		9 20	1032	5 32	6 40	8 4
Storeton	4 13			6 33		Sig.	8 36	9 5		a		9 25	1037	5 37	6 45	8 4
Upton	4 18		6 15	6 40		6 54	8 41	9 10		9 41		9 30	1042	5 42	6 50	8 5
Bidston 352	4 23		6 20	6 45		7 0	8 46	9 15		9 46		9 35	1047	5 47	6 55	8 5
Birkenhead Docks	5 1		6c31	7 1		8 1	9 1			10 1					7 20	9 3
Birkenhead Park	5 4		6c34	7 4		8 4	9 4			10 4					7 23	9 3
״ (Hamilton Sq.)	5 11		6c43	7 11		8 11	9 11			1013					7 35	9 4
L'pool (James St.).arr.	5 15		6c45	7 15		8 15	9 15			1017					7 39	9 4
״ (Cen., L. L.) ״	5 17		6c47	7 17		8 17	9 17			1019					7 42	9 5
Liscard and Poulton 352							8 49	9 18		9 49					6 58	9
Seacombe ....arr.	4 30		6 26	6 51		7 6	8 53	9 22		9 53		9 41	1053	5 53	7 2	9
Liverpool (Lan. Stage) ״	4 51		6 36	7 6		7 21	9 6	9 36		10 6		10 6	11 6	6 6	7 21	9 1

For other Trains between Bidston and Seacombe, see page 355. **b** Saturdays only. **c** Except Saturdays. * Connah's Quay and Shotton.

August 1898

September 1925

WREXHAM, HOPE, CONNAH'S QUAY, BIDSTON, BIRKENHEAD, and LIVERPOOL.—L. & N. E.

Miles	Down.	Week Days: mrn	mrn	mrn	mrn	mrn		noon		aft	aft	aft	aft
	Wrexham (Central)...dep.	6 40		7 38	Through Train, Chester to Seacombe.	9 40		Saturdays only.		1242	1 35	2 38	
¼	״ (Exchange)	6 43		7 41		9 43				1245	1 38	2 41	
2¼	Gwersyllt	6 48		7 46		9 49				1251	1 45	2 47	
4¼	Cefn-y-bedd	6 52		7 50		9 53				1255	1 49	2 51	
5	Caergwrle Castle and Wells	6 55		7 53		9 56				1258	1 52	2 54	
5¾	Hope Village	6 59		7 56		10 0				1 2	1 55	2 57	
7¼	Pen-y-ffordd **D**	7 4		8 1		10 8				1 7	2 0	3 2	
7½	**Hope** (Exchange) 405	7 7		8 4		10 11				1 10			
8¾	Buckley Junction	7 11		8 8		10 16		12 0		1 15	2 8	3 7	
10¼	Hawarden....[395, & below	7 17		8 13		10 21		12 5		1 20	2 13	3 12	4 15
13	**Connah's Quay C**390, arr.	7 22		8 18		10 26		12 10		1 25	2 18	3 17	4 20
20	Chester (Nthgate) arr.	7 51		8 51		10 55		12 41		1 56	2 38	3 46	
58¾	935 Manchester (Cen.) ״	10 0		1045		12 58				4 15		6 3	
—	828 Chester (Nthgate) dep.	7 0	7 35		8 25	9 50		11 45		1 0		3A0	4 0
—	**Connah's Quay** ....dep.	7 24	8 3	8 19	8 48	10 28		12 12		1 28	Saturdays only.	3 21	4 21
—	Hawarden Bridge Halt			8 21		10 30		12 14		1 30		3 23	4 23
16¾	Burton Point **B**		8 10			10 37		12 19		1 37		3 30	4 30
19	Neston and Parkgate	7 36	8 17	8 33	9 0	10 44		12 26		1 44		3 37	4 35
21½	Heswall Hills	7 42	8 23	8 39	9 6	10 50		12 32		1 50		3 43	4 41
23	Storeton, for Barnston	7 46	8 27	8 43		10 54		12 36		1 54		3 47	4 45
25¼	Upton	7 51	8 32	8 48		10 59		12 41		1 59		3 52	4 50
27½	**Bidston** 534	7V55	8V36			11V3		12V45		2V4		3V56	4V54
28¼	535 Birkenhead Docks arr.	8 9	8 52			11b17		1 29		2b22		4 22	5 19
29½	״ Park... ״	8 12	8 55			11b20		1 32		2b25		4 25	5 22
30¼	״ (Hamilton Sq.) ״	8 20	9 4			11 32		1 42		2c32		4 32	5 32
31½	**Liverpool** (James St.) ״	8 23	9 7			11 35		1 45		2c35		4 35	5 35
32	״ (Cen., L. L.) ״	8 25	9 9			11 37		1 47		2c37		4 37	5 37
28¾	Liscard & Poulton 534					11V8		12V50		2V10		4V1	4V58
30¾	**Seacombe & Egremont** arr.	8 3	8 44	9 0	9 26	11 12		12 54		2 14		4 5	5 3
31	**Liverpool** (Lan. Stage) ״	8 16	8 56	9 16	9 36	11 21		1 6		2 26		4 16	5 16

Down.	Week Days: aft	aft	aft		aft	aft	aft	aft					Sundays: mrn		aft		
Wrexham (Central)...dep.	4 5	4 30	5 23		7 10	9 0		10 35					8 15		5 10		
״ (Exchange)	4 8	4 33	5 26		7 13	9 3	Except Saturdays.										
Gwersyllt	4 13	4 38	5 32		7 18	9 10		10 42					8 21		5 16		
Cefn-y-bedd	4 17	4 42	5 36		7 22	9 14		10 46					8 27		5 23		
Caergwrle Castle and Wells	4 20	4 45	5 39		7 24	9 17		10 49					8 30		5 25		
Hope Village	4 23	4 48	5 43		7 27	9 20		10 53					8 37		5 31		
Pen-y-ffordd **D**	4 28	4 53	5 48		7 32	9 25		10 58					8 44		5 38		
Hope (Exchange) 405	4 31	4 55	5 51		7 35	9 28											
Buckley Junction	4 35	4 59	5 56		7 39	9 32	10 5	11 4					8 49		5 44		
Hawarden....[395, & below	4 41	5 4	6 1		7 44	9 37	1010	11 9					8 57		5 51		
Connah's Quay C390, arr.	4 46	5 9	6 6		7 49	9 42	1015	11 14					9 2		5 56		
Chester (Nthgate) arr.	5 8	5 38	6 42		8 24	10 43	1043	11 45					9 30		6 26		
935 Manchester (Cen.) ״	8 17	8 17			1018										8 50		
828 Chester (Nthgate) dep.			5 45		7 28	9 15							8 30		5 30		
Connah's Quay ....dep.	Saturdays only.	Except Saturdays.	6 9		7 50	9 44		Saturdays only.					9 5		5 59		
Hawarden Bridge Halt			6 11		7 52	9 46							9 7		6 1		
Burton Point **B**			6 19		8 0	9 53							9 15		6 9		
Neston and Parkgate			6 26		8 6	10 1							9 22		6 16		
Heswall Hills			6 32		8 13	10 7							9 28		6 22		
Storeton, for Barnston			6 36		8 16	10 11											
Upton			6 41		8 21	10 16							9 37		6 31		
Bidston 534			6V45		8V25	10V21							9V42		6V36		
535 Birkenhead Docks arr.			7 22		8 59	10 37									7 20		
״ Park... ״			7 25		9 2	10 40									7 24		
״ (Hamilton Sq.) ״			7 32		9 12	10 53									7 13		
Liverpool (James St.) ״			7 35		9 15	10 56									7 16		
״ (Cen., L. L.) ״			7 37		9 17	10 58									7 18		
Liscard & Poulton 534			6V50		8V30	10V26							9V47		6V41		
Seacombe & Egremont arr.			6 54		8 34	10 30							9 51		6 45		
Liverpool (Lan. Stage) ״			7 6		8 46	10 46							10 6		6 56		

A Leaves at 2 10 aft. on Saturdays.
B Station for Burton and Puddington.
b 5 minutes later on Saturdays.
C Connah's Quay and Shotton.
c 10 minutes later on Saturdays.
D Station for Leeswood.
V Stops when required to set down from Upton and beyond.

CONNAH'S QUAY, BLACON, and CHESTER.—L. & N. E.

Miles		Week Days: mrn	mrn	mrn	mrn	mrn		aft	aft	aft S	aft E	aft	aft S	aft E	aft	aft	aft	aft	aft S				Sundays: mrn	mrn		aft	aft			
	Connah's Quay & Shotton¶ dep	6 15	7 30	8 30	9 0	1035		12 20	1 33	2 20	2 33	3 25	4 47	5 12	5 47	6 20	8 5	1020	1130				9 10	11 5		6 5	9 25			
3½	Saughall	6 27	7 40	8 40		1044		12 30	1 45	2 27	2 44	3 35	4 57	5 27	5 59	6 31	8 13	1032	1137				9 19	1115		6 15	9 35			
5¼	Blacon		7 45	8 45		1049		12 35	1 50	2 32	2 49	3 40	5 2	5 32	6 4	6 36	8 18	1037					9 24	1120		6 20	9 40			
6½	**Chester** (Liverpool Road)	6 33	7 49	8 49	9 12	1053		12 39	1 54	2 36	2 53	3 44	5 6	5 36	6 8	6 40	8 22	1041	1143											
7	״ (Northgate) **G** 935, arr.	6 35	7 51	8 51	9 14	1055		12 41	1 56	2 38	2 55	3 46	5 8	5 38	6 10	6 42	8 24	1043	1145				9 30	1123		6 26	9 46			

E Except Saturdays. **G** About ¼ mile to General Station. **S** Sats. only. ¶ "Halts" at Hawarden Bridge and Welsh Road between Connah's Quay and Saughall.

Table 111

SEACOMBE, NEW BRIGHTON, BIRKENHEAD and WREXHAM

Week Days | **Sundays**

(Timetable data — Table 111, upper section: Seacombe & Egremont dep, Liscard and Poulton, New Brighton dep, Liverpool dep, Birkenhead A, Bidston, Upton, Storeton for Barnston, Heswall Hills, Neston and Parkgate, Burton Point, Hawarden Bridge Halt, Connah's Quay C, Buckley Junction, Hope (Exchange), Pen-y-ffordd D, Hope Village, Caergwrle Castle and Wells, Cefn-y-bedd, Gwersyllt, Wrexham (Exchange), (Central) arr.)

(Timetable data — Table 111, lower section: Wrexham (Central) dep, (Exchange), Gwersyllt, Cefn-y-bedd, Caergwrle Castle and Wells, Hope Village, Pen-y-ffordd D, Hope (Exchange), Buckley Junction, Hawarden, Connah's Quay C arr / dep, Hawarden Bridge Halt, Burton Point, Neston and Parkgate, Heswall Hills, Storeton for Barnston, Upton, Bidston, Birkenhead A arr, Liverpool arr, New Brighton arr, Liscard and Poulton, Seacombe & Egremont arr.)

A Hamilton Square. **B** Station for Burton and Puddington. **C** Connah's Quay and Shotton. **D** Station for Leeswood. **E** or **E** Except Saturdays. **H** Central (Low Level). **¤** Arr. 3 minutes earlier. **L** 3 mins. later on Saturdays. **N** Arr. 9 mins. earlier. **S** or **S** Saturdays only. **u** 9 mins. later on Saturdays. **V** 2 mins. earlier on Saturdays. **Y** 2 mins. later on Saturdays. **Z** 8 mins. earlier on Saturdays.

‡ 7 mins. earlier on Saturdays   For OTHER TRAINS between Hawarden Bridge Halt and Connah's Quay and Shotton, see Table 112.

Both are from September 1948

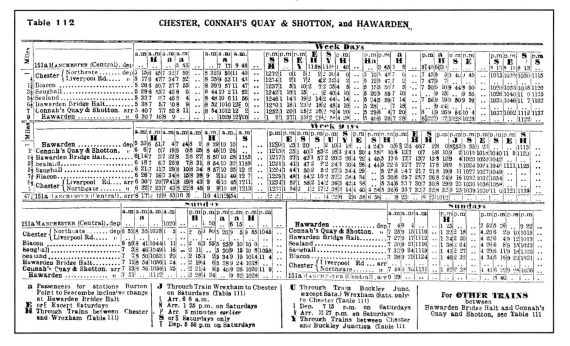

Table 112

CHESTER, CONNAH'S QUAY & SHOTTON, and HAWARDEN

Week Days | **Sundays**

(Timetable data — Table 112: Manchester (Central) dep, Chester (Northgate / Liverpool Rd.) dep, Blacon, Saughall, Sealand, Hawarden Bridge Halt, Connah's Quay & Shotton arr, Hawarden; and reverse direction.)

a Passengers for stations Burton Point to Seacombe inclusive change at Hawarden Bridge Halt. **E** or **E** Except Saturdays. **H** Through Trains between Chester and Wrexham (Table 111). **J** Through Train Wrexham to Chester on Saturdays (Table 111). **N** Arr. 6 8 a.m. **P** Arr. 3 minutes earlier. **S** or **S** Saturdays only. **T** Dep. 5 58 p.m. on Saturdays. **U** Through Train Buckley Junc. except Sats.) Wrexham (Sats. only) to Chester (Table 111). **L** Dep. 7 15 p.m. on Saturdays. **V** Arr. 11 27 p.m. on Saturdays. **Y** Through Trains between Chester and Buckley Junction (Table 111).

For OTHER TRAINS between Hawarden Bridge Halt and Connah's Quay and Shotton, see Table 111

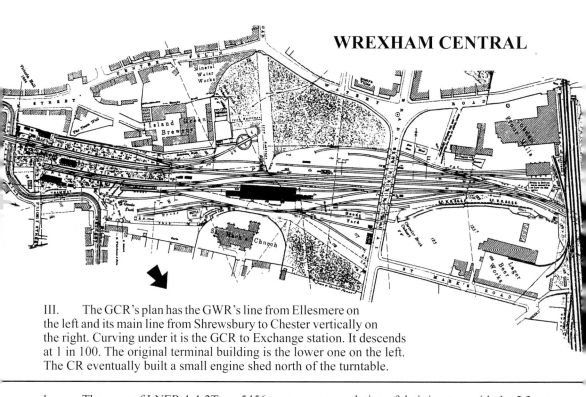

III.   The GCR's plan has the GWR's line from Ellesmere on the left and its main line from Shrewsbury to Chester vertically on the right. Curving under it is the GCR to Exchange station. It descends at 1 in 100. The original terminal building is the lower one on the left. The CR eventually built a small engine shed north of the turntable.

1.   The crew of LNER 4-4-2T no. 5456 pose upon completion of their journey with the 5.3pm from Connah's Quay & Shotton on 8th April 1939. The route from Wrexham General had been doubled in 1888. The spire of St. Marks Church is prominent. (C.A.Appleton/J.K.Williams)

2. The tower of St. Giles Church is evident in this view in the opposite direction on 10th August 1953. At the head of the 3.55pm to Seacombe is class C13 4-4-2T no. 67412. The two original bay platforms are on the left. (H.C.Casserley)

3. The original terminal building is on the left and under the footbridge can be seen the window of the ex-GCR Central South box. Platform 5 is out of view and was a little used bay. (LOSA)

4.　　A DMU is about to turn left into the platform to terminate, having worked from Chester Northgate on 12th March 1966. The massive goods shed and extensive yard were in use until 7th December 1964. There had been a 7-ton crane present. The 56-lever box was in use until 19th August 1973 and was rescued for use on the new GCR. (J.M.Tolson/F.Hornby coll.)

5.　　Only a fragment of platform 3 remained to be photographed on 13th December 1997. No. 4 had usually received trains from Ellesmere on the former GWR route. The branch seen was singled in August 1973. (J.Whitehouse)

6.   A closer view on the same day includes the tiny shelter and random rubble. By that time the service was to Bidston only. Staffing had ceased on 7th February 1972. The descent had an 8mph speed limit. (J.Whitehouse)

For other views of this station, see picture nos 107 to 120 in our *Oswestry to Whitchurch* album.

7.   A new terminus was opened on 23rd November 1998, 400 yards west of the previous one. Its tall entrance hall was styled to match the adjacent buildings in the spacious shopping development. It is seen in September 2008. (Milepost 92½)

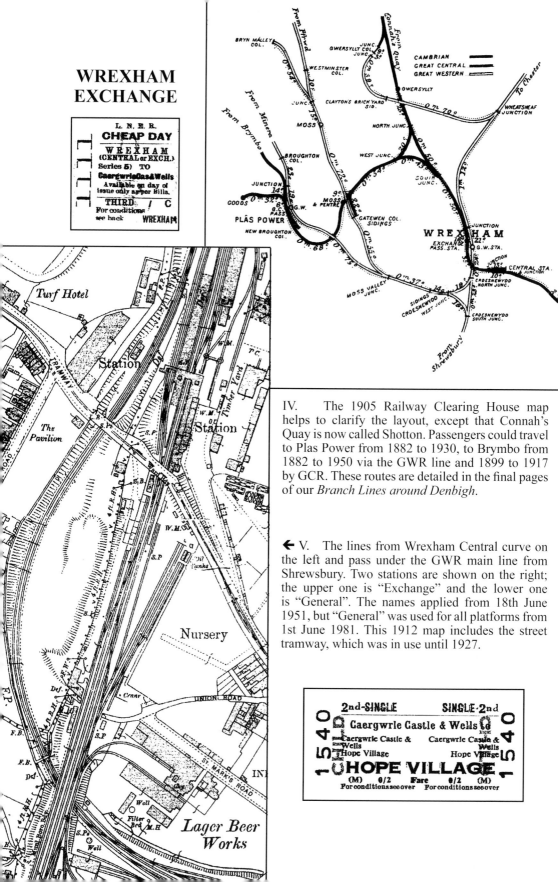

WREXHAM EXCHANGE

L. N. E. R.
CHEAP DAY
WREXHAM
(CENTRAL or EXCH.)
Series 5) TO
Caergwrle Cas & Wells
Available on day of
issue only as per Bills.
THIRD / **C**
For conditions
see back **WREXHAM**

IV.　　The 1905 Railway Clearing House map helps to clarify the layout, except that Connah's Quay is now called Shotton. Passengers could travel to Plas Power from 1882 to 1930, to Brymbo from 1882 to 1950 via the GWR line and 1899 to 1917 by GCR. These routes are detailed in the final pages of our *Branch Lines around Denbigh*.

← V.　　The lines from Wrexham Central curve on the left and pass under the GWR main line from Shrewsbury. Two stations are shown on the right; the upper one is "Exchange" and the lower one is "General". The names applied from 18th June 1951, but "General" was used for all platforms from 1st June 1981. This 1912 map includes the street tramway, which was in use until 1927.

2nd-SINGLE　　**SINGLE-2nd**
1540　　**Caergwrle Castle & Wells**　　**1540**
Caergwrle Castle &　　Caergwrle Castle &
Wells　　Wells
Hope Village　　Hope Village
CHOPE VILLAGE
(M) 0/2　　Fare　　0/2 (M)
For conditions see over　　For conditions see over

8. Both GCR platforms were curved, whereas all three through ones on the GWR side were almost straight. There were also two bays at the south end, that side. (LOSA)

9. A train destined for Wrexham Central is arriving behind ex-GCR class N5 no. 9289 on 9th May 1949. The assorted coaches are of some antiquity. Ex-GWR stock stands at platform 2. (LOSA)

10. The 15.34 Bidston to Wrexham Central was recorded on 6th June 1982. The platform on the left was not used after August 1973. Major station improvements are evident in the next photograph; compare the views from the same location. (T.Heavyside)

11. No. 150280 is working the 08.31 Bidston to Wrexham Central on 16th March 2013 and is about to face the steep climb. The Wrexham & Shropshire Railway provided a direct service to London from platform 3 in 2008 to 2011. (P.D.Shannon)

Wrexham General is illustrated in pictures 77 to 88 in our *Shrewsbury to Chester* album.

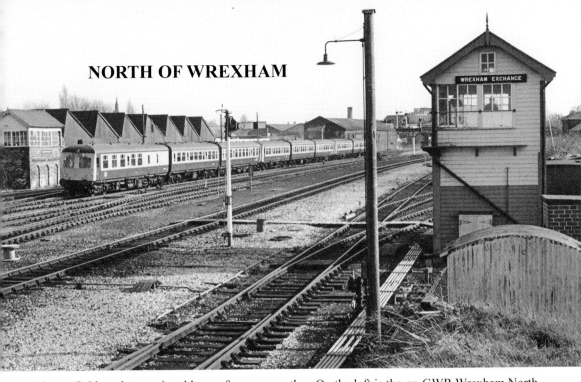

NORTH OF WREXHAM

12.   Seldom do two signal boxes face one another. On the left is the ex-GWR Wrexham North, which had a 41-lever frame and was in use from about 1883 until 16th March 1986. Nearer is the 1912 GCR 28-lever box, which lasted until 27th March 1988. It was later moved to the preserved GCR and the district was controlled from a modernised box, south of the station. A train of three DMU sets ends near the goods shed. The yard closed on 2nd March 1970. The train is on the line to Chester. (J.Whitehouse)

13.   This and the previous photograph were taken on 21st April 1984. Heads are projecting from the "Conway Crusader" as it is accelerated towards Birkenhead by no. 40122. It will travel via Shotton and Bidston and is approaching Gwersyllt. (J.Whitehouse)

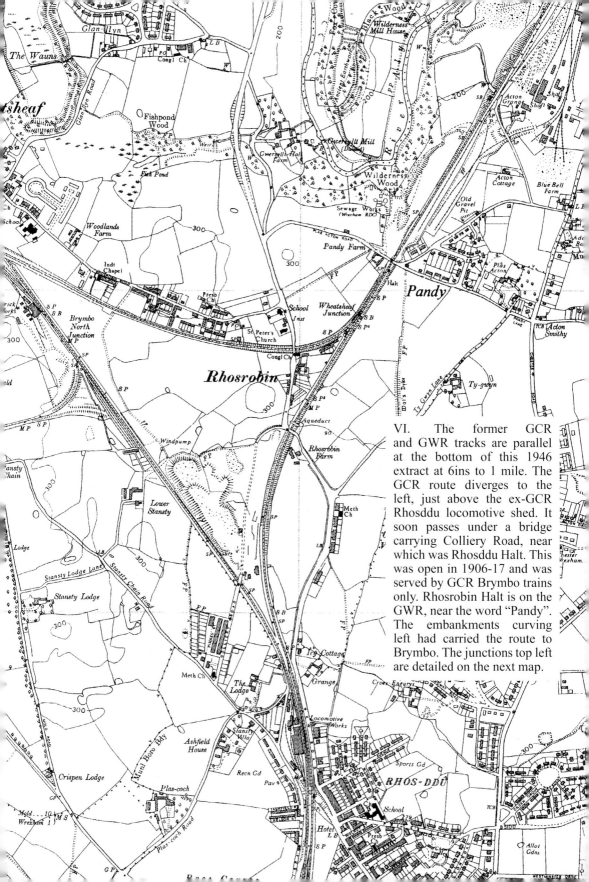

VI. The former GCR and GWR tracks are parallel at the bottom of this 1946 extract at 6ins to 1 mile. The GCR route diverges to the left, just above the ex-GCR Rhosddu locomotive shed. It soon passes under a bridge carrying Colliery Road, near which was Rhosddu Halt. This was open in 1906-17 and was served by GCR Brymbo trains only. Rhosrobin Halt is on the GWR, near the word "Pandy". The embankments curving left had carried the route to Brymbo. The junctions top left are detailed on the next map.

14.   The WM&CQR Rhosddu shed is seen in GCR days. In attendance are nos 79, 403, 406 and others. A six-road building replaced it in 1912 and a ramped coal stage was provided. (R.M.Casserley coll.)

15.   The shed was photographed on 29th April 1956 and on display were nos 84003, 40086 and 69362. Closure came on 4th January 1960 and the stock was transferred to the former GWR shed at Croes Newydd, south of the station. See pictures 71 to 74 in our *Shrewsbury to Chester* album. The LMR code was 6E in 1949-58 and 84K finally. The allocation was 29 in 1950. (G.Adams/M.J.Stretton coll.)

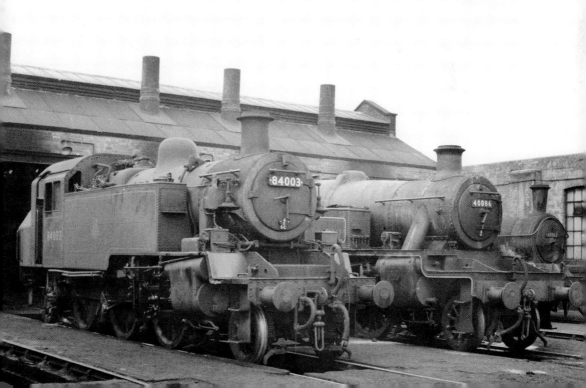

VII.   The line from Wrexham to Buckley Junction is lower right to top left and it was doubled in 1885. The 1909 survey is at 15ins to 1 mile. The 21-lever Brymbo South Box was in use in about 1888 to 1931. North Box had 44 levers and lasted from 1885 until 1971. Note that there were three tracks at the lower right corner and no junction. The speed limit on the curves was 10mph. Near North Junction is Claytons Brickworks. The Wheatsheaf branch seldom carried passengers, but was used mainly for coal and clay products from the Brymbo area to the Wirral docks.

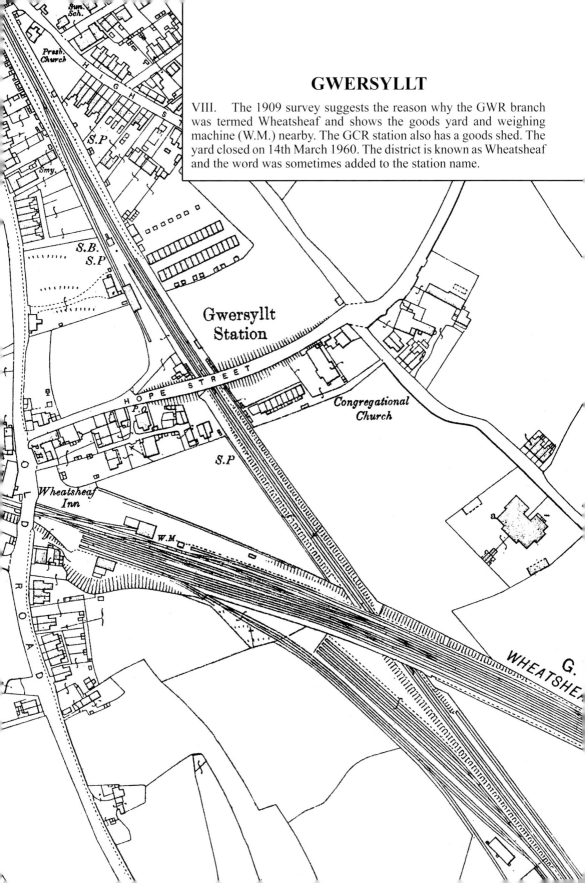

GWERSYLLT

VIII.   The 1909 survey suggests the reason why the GWR branch was termed Wheatsheaf and shows the goods yard and weighing machine (W.M.) nearby. The GCR station also has a goods shed. The yard closed on 14th March 1960. The district is known as Wheatsheaf and the word was sometimes added to the station name.

16. The brick structure formed the original station and the single storey building was created by the GCR. Steps were provided to both platforms. The population had reached 4551 by 1901. (LOSA)

17. Ex-GCR 0-6-2T class N5 no. 69267 runs in from the north in May 1949. The goods shed and the signal box were just beyond the left border. The frame had 14 levers and was worked from 1885 to 1945. (M.Whitehouse coll.)

18.　　No. 40109 runs through with cement hoppers from the Tunnel Cement Works at Buckley on 18th September 1980. All traces of the goods yard had long gone, but rural life was still evident on the right. (T.Heavyside)

19.　　Fresh shelters are present as no. 150252 departs for Bidston on 25th October 2010. The Lidl supermarket on the left apparently generates steady rail traffic. The train will climb at 1 in 80 to run near Windy Hill. (A.C.Hartless)

CEFN-Y-BEDD

IX. The 1912 issue has the GCR line on the left and on the right is the mineral line serving Llay Hall Colliery to the south and Hope Colliery, to the north. The route opened in September 1877 and closed in 1966, when Llay Main Colliery shut. Llay Hall Firebrick Works had been nearby, until about 1910. The paper mill shown had earlier been a rope works. The nearby dots and dashes represent the county boundary, this being in the River Alyn. The lengthy goods yard closed on 14th May 1964.

C.S.

G.P

Well

Shaft

Shaft

S.P

Old Colliery

Sluice

S.P

C

S.B.

Weir

Sl

Union & R.D.Bdy.

W.M.

Station

Sunnyside

Hope Paper Mills (Disused)

C.R.

Mill Race

S.P

Well

S.P

M.S

Hollybush Inn

G.P

P.O.

Cefn-y-bedd Mill (Corn)

F.B.

Little Liverpool

M.S

Mold........7
Wrexham....4

Gwastad Bridge

20. The date is 3rd March 1956 and class N5 0-6-2T no. 69281 runs in from the north. There had been a 14-lever box near the signal until 1945. (Bentley coll.)

21. The down side building had been created by the WM&CQR in its "Wirral" style, as a replacement for the original basic structure. The fine gardens and lowly oil lamp are seen in August 1959. (Bentley coll.)

22. Passengers still had to use the foot crossing to access the up platform when this photograph was taken on 23rd May 1997. Staff had been withdrawn on 20th April 1969. No. 153313 departs north into the woodland. The platforms were limited to four coaches by that time. (A.C.Hartless)

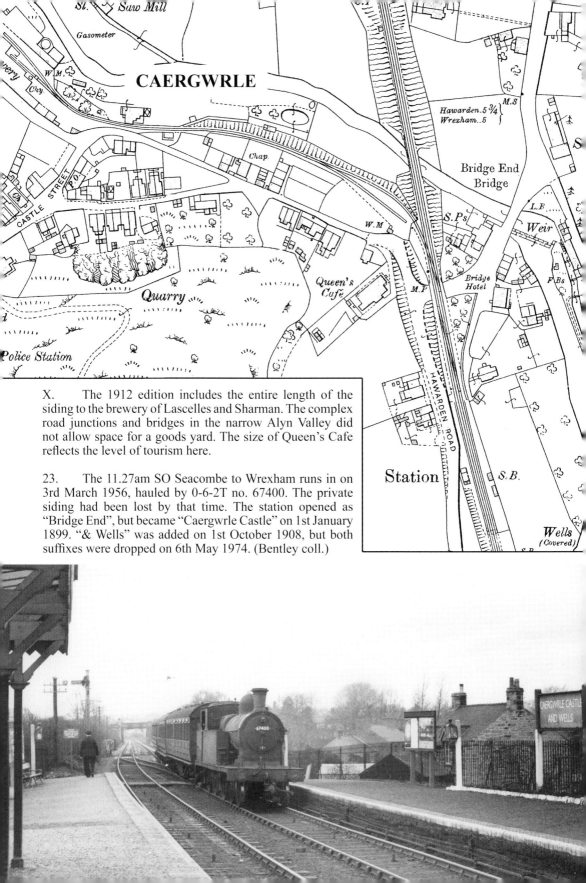

CAERGWRLE

Hawarden..5¾
Wrexham..5

Bridge End
Bridge

Weir

S.Ps

Bridge
Hotel

Station

Wells
(Covered)

X.   The 1912 edition includes the entire length of the siding to the brewery of Lascelles and Sharman. The complex road junctions and bridges in the narrow Alyn Valley did not allow space for a goods yard. The size of Queen's Cafe reflects the level of tourism here.

23.   The 11.27am SO Seacombe to Wrexham runs in on 3rd March 1956, hauled by 0-6-2T no. 67400. The private siding had been lost by that time. The station opened as "Bridge End", but became "Caergwrle Castle" on 1st January 1899. "& Wells" was added on 1st October 1908, but both suffixes were dropped on 6th May 1974. (Bentley coll.)

24.   The platforms were longer here than elsewhere, probably due to excursion traffic to the castle and wells. Both platforms took four coaches in the 1990s. The box had 20 levers and was worked from 1885 until 28th November 1982. The box's name was "Caergwrle Castle Station" from 1898 to 1972. The castle was near the left border of the map. (LOSA)

25.   Rolled steel is in transit from Port Talbot to Shotton for finishing on 23rd October 1991. Leading is no. 37350, the class pioneer as no. D6700. Behind it is no. 37505 *British Steel Workington*. The former was saved by the National Railway Museum. (A.C.Hartless)

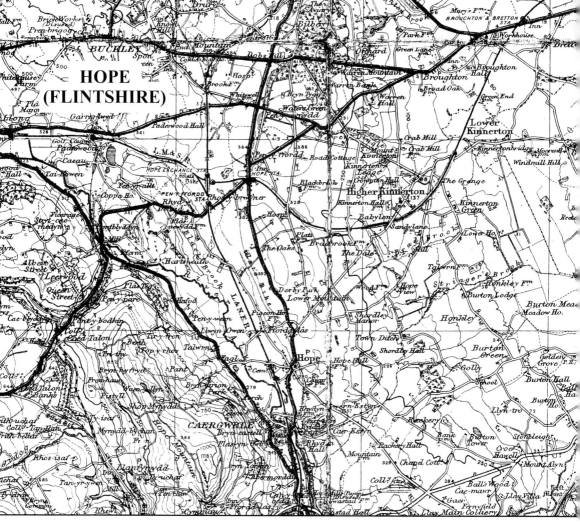

XI. The 1927 edition at 1ins to 1 mile has Hope station only about ½ mile north of Caergwrle. The small village is about ¼ mile from its station, while the LMS Hope station is 1½ miles to the north. Three other stations can be found within ½ mile, while Buckley's is one mile to the north of them. To the left of it is the start of the goods-only route to Connah's Quay, known in its early years as the Buckley Railway.

26. A snap from a southbound train on 10th August 1953 records well tended gardens, together with one low oil lamp and two high ones. As at the two stations to the south, there was no footbridge or subway. (H.C.Casserley)

27.   The 12.34pm Chester Northgate to Wrexham Central service is pictured on 3rd March 1956, headed by class C13 4-4-2T no. 67430, a type introduced in 1898. The signal box had 17 levers and was open from 1885 until 1st August 1965. A van is in the goods yard, which closed on 4th May 1964. (Bentley coll.)

XII.   The 1912 survey shows the station name in use from 1st January 1899 until 6th May 1974. Initially, it had been Caergwrle. The crane (C) was rated at one ton.

28.   No. 150252 departs north on 25th October 2010 as a representative of the cleaning contractor maintains tidiness. He has the door open for new information. Platform 1 takes three coaches, while no. 2 can cope with four. (A.C.Hartless)

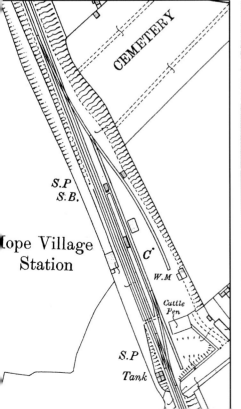

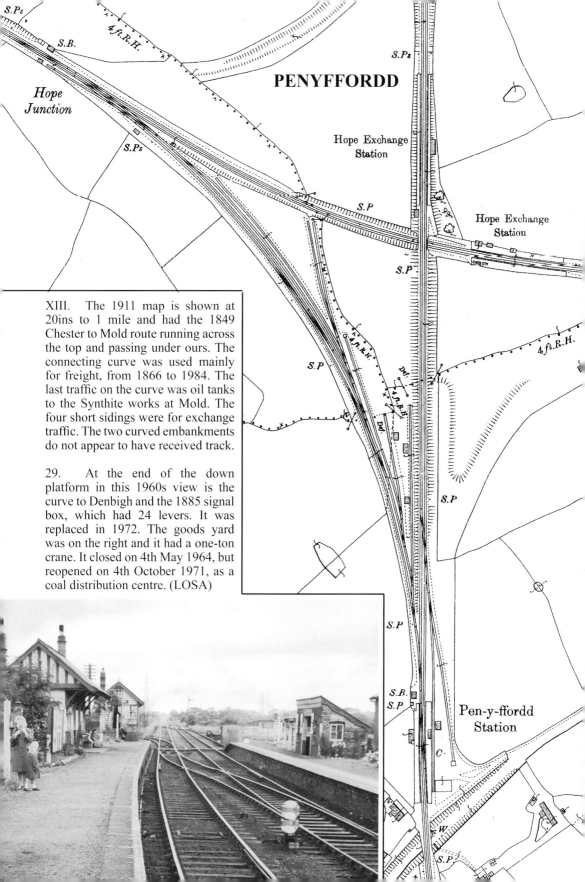

PENYFFORDD

Hope
Junction

S.Ps

S.B.

4 ft.R.H.

S.Ps

S.Ps

S.P

Hope Exchange
Station

Hope Exchange
Station

S.P

S.P

4 ft.R.H.

S.P

A.P.R.H.

S.P

Def.

4 ft.R.H.

Def.

S.P

S.P

S.B.
S.P

C.

Pen-y-ffordd
Station

W.

S.P

XIII. The 1911 map is shown at 20ins to 1 mile and had the 1849 Chester to Mold route running across the top and passing under ours. The connecting curve was used mainly for freight, from 1866 to 1984. The last traffic on the curve was oil tanks to the Synthite works at Mold. The four short sidings were for exchange traffic. The two curved embankments do not appear to have received track.

29. At the end of the down platform in this 1960s view is the curve to Denbigh and the 1885 signal box, which had 24 levers. It was replaced in 1972. The goods yard was on the right and it had a one-ton crane. It closed on 4th May 1964, but reopened on 4th October 1971, as a coal distribution centre. (LOSA)

30.   The new signal box opened on 17th December 1972 and was photographed on 19th April 1986. It had 25 levers and was still in use in 2013. A hood is up as no. 142043 leaves for Wrexham Central. Both platforms were suitable for three coaches. (J.Whitehouse)

31.   The foot crossing is seen again, but with a single car, no. 153316. The station had been opened as "Hope Junction", but became "Penyffordd for Hope" in 1877. "Penyffordd for Leeswood" was the name from 1st March 1913 until 1974. Two hyphens were used from 1896 until 1961. (M.J.Stretton)

HOPE EXCHANGE HIGH LEVEL

32.　　The sign says it all as LNER class C3 4-4-2T runs south in 1948, except that reference to the L&NW was 25 years out of date. For the Low Level platforms and the connecting footpath, see pictures 35 and 36 in *Branch Lines around Denbigh*. There was no external access to the platforms, which were in use from 18th November 1867 until 1st September 1958. (R.M.Casserley coll.)

SOUTH OF BUCKLEY

33.　　Almost ¾ mile from Buckley was this cement works. Its sidings are on the west side of the line, near Padeswood Hall. The 200ft tower is a major feature in the landscape, having been an important part of the works since its completion in about 1950 by Tunnel Portland Cement. (D.Southern)

34.   The works despatched cement by rail until 1990 and coal was brought to it this way from July 1996. Main line locomotives have since undertaken the shunting and thus the works shunters have gone. Most had been Rustons, although a Sentinel is visible here. (D.Southern)

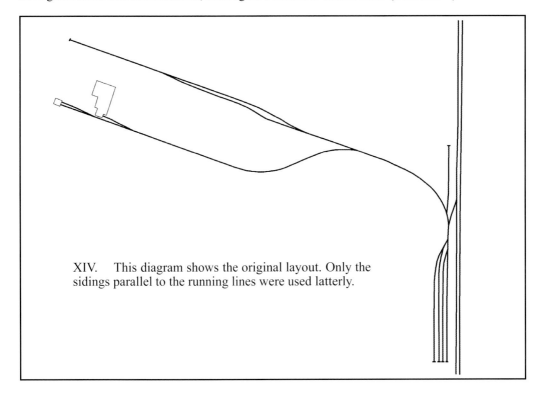

XIV.   This diagram shows the original layout. Only the sidings parallel to the running lines were used latterly.

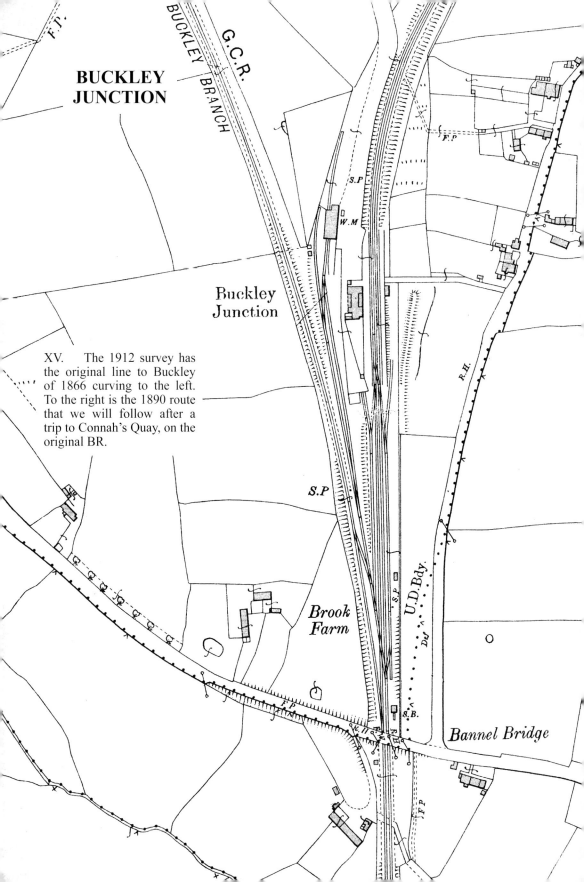

BUCKLEY JUNCTION

G.C.R.

F.P.

BUCKLEY BRANCH

Buckley
Junction

S.P

W.M

F.P

XV.   The 1912 survey has
the original line to Buckley
of 1866 curving to the left.
To the right is the 1890 route
that we will follow after a
trip to Connah's Quay, on the
original BR.

R.H.

S.P.

Brook
Farm

U.D.Bdy.

Def

S.P

F.P

S.B.

Bannel Bridge

F.P

35.   This northward view is from the bridge near the bottom of the map. The 1885 box had 20 levers and was in use until 16th February 1972. It is seen in about 1960. (LOSA)

36.   A view from about 1934 features class C13 4-4-2T no. 6056 southbound. Also included is the small cattle dock, with end-loading facilities. The shelter on the right was of yellow brick construction. (R.M.Casserley coll.)

37.   Running through with hoppers on 13th April 1957 is BR no. 44058, an ex-LMS class 4F 0-6-0. Back in 1938, there had been 13 private sidings in this vicinity. (R.M.Casserley coll.)

BUCKLEY

38.   The station was unstaffed from 20th April 1969 and the goods yard was closed on 4th October 1971. The suffix "Junction" was dropped on 6th May 1974. It is 6th April 1991 and no. 142001 departs forming the 13.41 Bidston to Wrexham. (A.C.Hartless)

Buckley Branch

XVI.   The line to Connah's Quay was built by a group of local industrialists and colliery owners, who wished to be free of tramway proprietors and their excessive charges. The Act was passed in June 1860 and traffic began in June 1862. Two locomotives and two vans were purchased by the Buckley Railway Company and users provided their own wagons. Gradients were as steep as 1 in 28 and curves were down to 2½ chains (50m). This 1906 extract is at 1ins to 1 mile and has the GCR line from Wrexham at the bottom. Buckley is near the centre and Connah's Quay at the top. The line between them is unclear, as it was only single track. However, the numerous cuttings and curves are evident. The line across the map can be studied in our *Branch Lines around Denbigh* album; it is marked "London Nth. Western Railway". The Brymbo Branch from Mold is lower left and Hawarden Bridge over the River Dee is top right. Dee Junction is above it, the line to Chester Northgate curving to the right and the one to New Brighton running to the top.

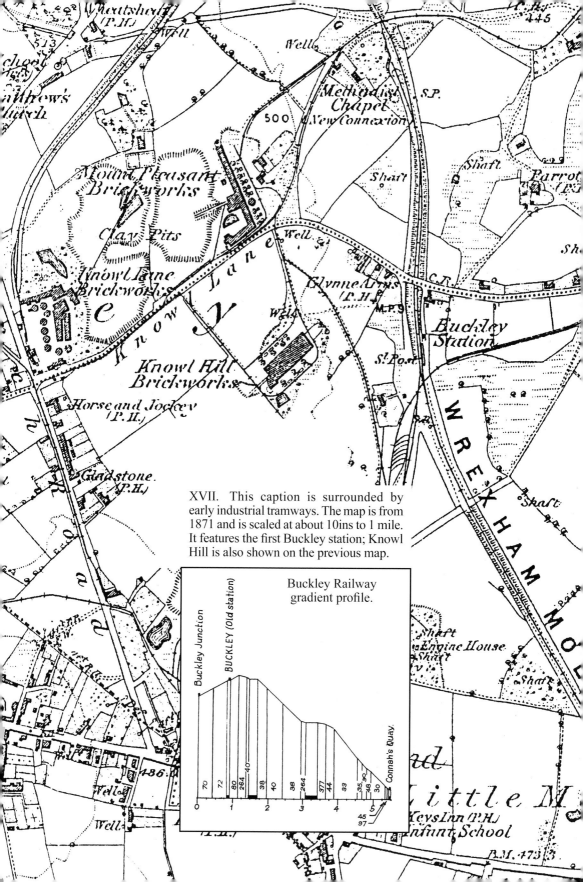

XVII. This caption is surrounded by early industrial tramways. The map is from 1871 and is scaled at about 10ins to 1 mile. It features the first Buckley station; Knowl Hill is also shown on the previous map.

Buckley Railway gradient profile.

39.   This is a southward view of the original station in May 1953, with a loading gauge behind the trees. The rodding tunnel had served a ground frame near the building in earlier years. (C.H.A.Townley)

40.   Mount Pleasant Colliery had been sunk in about 1768 and was to the east of Buckley. It shared a siding with the Standard Brick & Terracotta Company. The 0-6-0T is WM&CQR no. 6 *Queen*; it had been built by Sharp Bros. with a tender, in 1846 and had been bought from the LNWR in 1872. (Bentley coll.)

41.　　This is the nearby siding of the SB&T Co. and the panorama is included to emphasise the industrial nature of the district. The works was active from 1886 to 1914 and later produced pipes. (A.Dudman coll.)

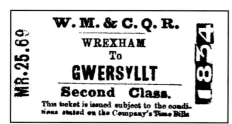

42.　　A northward view of the first Buckley station in 1957 includes the chimney of the Drury Brickworks. It was productive from 1874 to 1976. (G.H.Platt)

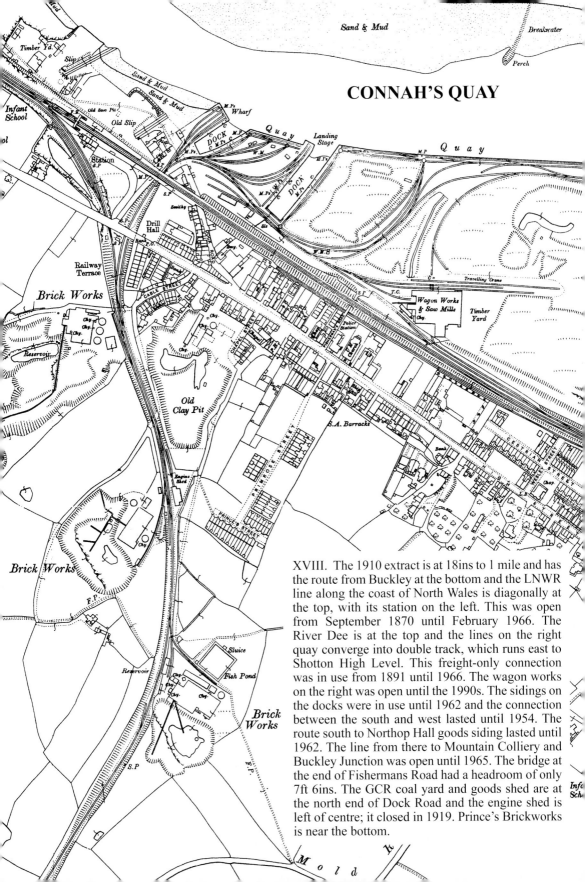

CONNAH'S QUAY

XVIII. The 1910 extract is at 18ins to 1 mile and has the route from Buckley at the bottom and the LNWR line along the coast of North Wales is diagonally at the top, with its station on the left. This was open from September 1870 until February 1966. The River Dee is at the top and the lines on the right quay converge into double track, which runs east to Shotton High Level. This freight-only connection was in use from 1891 until 1966. The wagon works on the right was open until the 1990s. The sidings on the docks were in use until 1962 and the connection between the south and west lasted until 1954. The route south to Northop Hall goods siding lasted until 1962. The line from there to Mountain Colliery and Buckley Junction was open until 1965. The bridge at the end of Fishermans Road had a headroom of only 7ft 6ins. The GCR coal yard and goods shed are at the north end of Dock Road and the engine shed is left of centre; it closed in 1919. Prince's Brickworks is near the bottom.

43.   A view from the LNWR in 1876 features the coal wharf, with coal boxes on wagons on the right. They may be small pottery wagons. The sails are probably being dried. (A.Dudman coll.)

44.   This photograph from 1949 includes the coal dock and 0-6-0ST class J62 no. E8200. It is on one of the 2½ chain curves. The former goods yard is on the right. (H.F.Wheeller/R.S.Carpenter)

45.   This is the junction on the approach to the docks on 2nd May 1953. The line on the left runs under the A548 main road to join the Chester-Rhyl route and was closed in 1954. The adjacent goods sidings were not used after 1st November 1952. (C.H.A.Townley)

46.   Seen on the same day are two signals on the main line, plus the dock lines branching out. In the background is Shotton Steel Works and the wide River Dee. The white fence is on the down platform of the station, which closed on 14th February 1966. (C.H.A.Townley)

For views of the main line, please see our *Chester to Rhyl* album, picture numbers 39 to 42.

47.   By the 1960s, diesels had taken over the dock shunting. No. D2388 is on one of the sharpest curves. The station name retained its apostrophe until nationalisation and so it appears in this album. The name was New Quay until about 1860 and the town was the largest in Flintshire in 2011. (T.Walsh coll.)

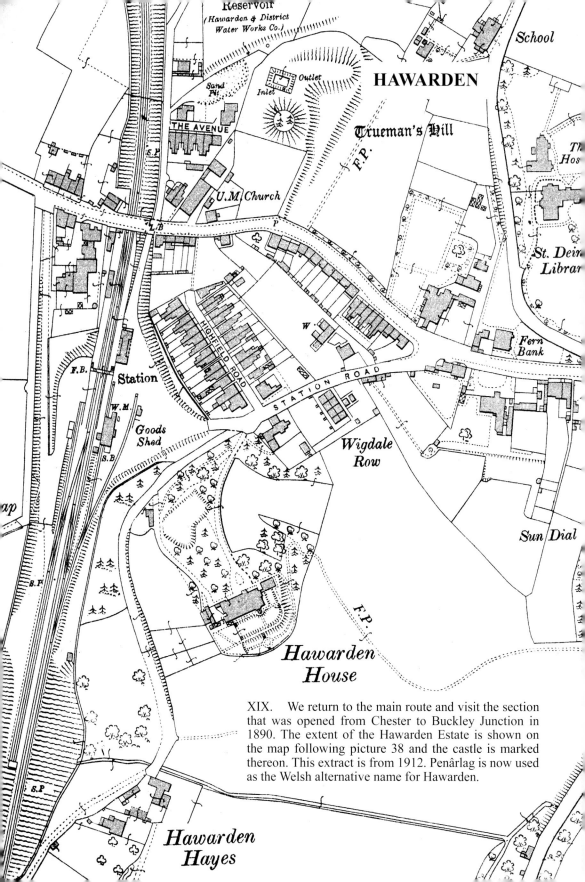

Reservoir
(Hawarden & District
Water Works Co.)

Sand Pit

THE AVENUE

S.P.

U.M.Church

L.B.

P

F.B.

Station

W.M.

Goods Shed

S.B.

S.P.

F.B.

S.P.

HIGHFIELD ROAD

STATION ROAD

Outlet

Inlet

HAWARDEN

Trueman's Hill

F.P.

School

St. Dein
Librar

Fern
Bank

W

Wigdale
Row

Sun Dial

F.P.

*Hawarden
House*

XIX.   We return to the main route and visit the section
that was opened from Chester to Buckley Junction in
1890. The extent of the Hawarden Estate is shown on
the map following picture 38 and the castle is marked
thereon. This extract is from 1912. Penârlag is now used
as the Welsh alternative name for Hawarden.

*Hawarden
Hayes*

48.   A southward view in about 1900 includes the outline of the signal box, which had 20 levers and was in use from 1890 until 2nd November 1979. Adjacent to it is the goods shed; the yard closed on 4th May 1964. (J.K.Williams coll.)

49.   Prime Minister Gladstone had lived nearby and there was much excursion traffic to view his home. Maybe this traffic justified the provision of a footbridge. There were 5372 residents in 1901 and 16,575 in 1961. (P.Laming coll.)

50.　　No. 150257 departs for Bidston on 25th October 2010 and runs near the long lengths of disused platform. Space for five coaches was retained on platform 1 and six on No. 2. The gradient from Buckley is 1 in 53 down and the train will continue down at 1 in 60 for one mile. It will pass the site of Aston Hall Junction where the line to the colliery of that name branched off. The box had 20 levers and was in use between about 1892 and 1920. Next was Wrights Bridge box for two sidings to brickworks. Its frame had 21 levers and was worked between 1901 and 1932. (A.C.Hartless)

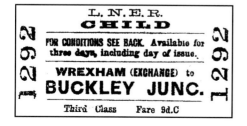

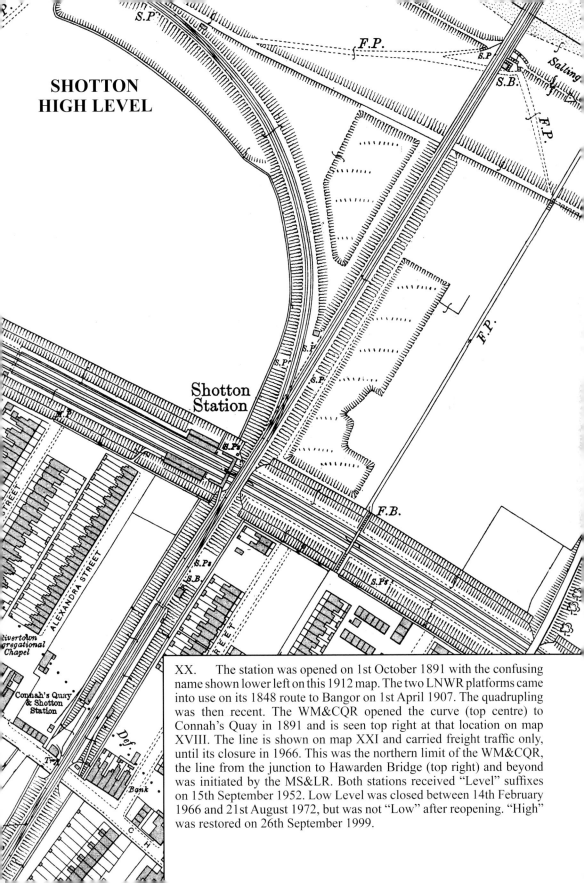

**SHOTTON
HIGH LEVEL**

Shotton
Station

XX.   The station was opened on 1st October 1891 with the confusing name shown lower left on this 1912 map. The two LNWR platforms came into use on its 1848 route to Bangor on 1st April 1907. The quadrupling was then recent. The WM&CQR opened the curve (top centre) to Connah's Quay in 1891 and is seen top right at that location on map XVIII. The line is shown on map XXI and carried freight traffic only, until its closure in 1966. This was the northern limit of the WM&CQR, the line from the junction to Hawarden Bridge (top right) and beyond was initiated by the MS&LR. Both stations received "Level" suffixes on 15th September 1952. Low Level was closed between 14th February 1966 and 21st August 1972, but was not "Low" after reopening. "High" was restored on 26th September 1999.

51. An early postcard shows the end of the 1 in 53 descent from Hawarden and that wooden platforms were used to minimise the weight on the embankment. (R.M.Casserley coll.)

52. The footpath between the two stations is featured in this southward view from 10th August 1953. Ex-LNER class C13 no. 67412 is passing Hawarden Bridge Junction Box, which was in use from about 1905 until 18th April 1971. (H.F.Wheeller/ R.S.Carpenter coll.)

For pictures of
LOW LEVEL
see nos 35 to 38
in our
Chester to Rhyl
album.

53.   No. 20039 leads, as empty steel wagons from Margam to Dee Marsh reach the end of the incline on 19th April 1986. Anti-graffiti ornamentation (left) is to be admired. Both platforms were for five cars. (J.Whitehouse)

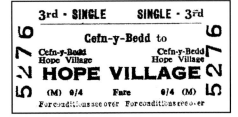

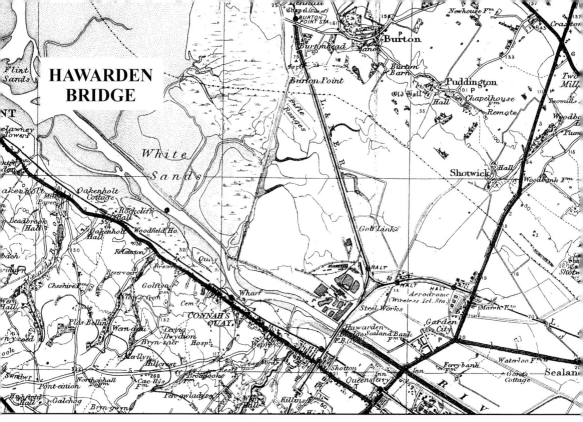

XXI.   The 1919 edition at 1ins to 1 mile includes John Summers Steel Works, but not the adjacent halt, as it did not open until 22nd September 1924. At the top of the triangle is Birkenhead Junction Golf Platform (1896 to 1927) and to the right of it is Chester Junction Golf Platform (1895-1927). They did not appear in public timetables. Just above centre are Rifle Ranges; a halt called "Sealand Rifle Range" was available nearby for military traffic from about 1923 to 1956; it was near the N of L&NER, but three miles from Sealand.

54.   The 11.27am Seacombe to Wrexham was recorded on 10th August 1953, with class C13 4-4-2T no. 67412 in charge. (H.C.Casserley)

55. Timetables show-
ed this as Hawarden
Bridge Halt until
1954, when the suffix
was dropped. This is
a northward view in
1958 and includes a
water tank at the end
of the left platform.
(LOSA)

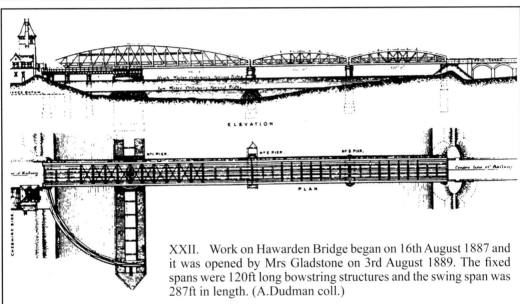

XXII. Work on Hawarden Bridge began on 16th August 1887 and
it was opened by Mrs Gladstone on 3rd August 1889. The fixed
spans were 120ft long bowstring structures and the swing span was
287ft in length. (A.Dudman coll.)

56. The swing span
and platform are at
the north end of the
bridge. Hawarden
Bridge Tower is pic-
tured in about 1960.
Near its top were
six signal levers and
the hydraulic con-
trol mechanism. The
bridge was last swung
for river traffic long
before the tower was
demolished in 1975.
(LOSA)

57.　No. 47227 has crossed Hawarden Bridge and is entering the station on 23rd August 1985. The train is the 06.25 Warrington Arpley to Dee Marsh Junction, via Wrexham, where it had to reverse. The train was carrying a typical mixture of empty scrap metal wagons for the steel works and timber wagons for Shotton Paper Company. (P.D.Shannon)

58.　The splendid bridge is seen from the north bank on 25th October 2010, looking towards the sea. The land end of the right span was shorter than that over the navigation channel and it was supported on rollers running on curved strips. Closure often delayed trains by up to 20 minutes. (A.C.Hartless)

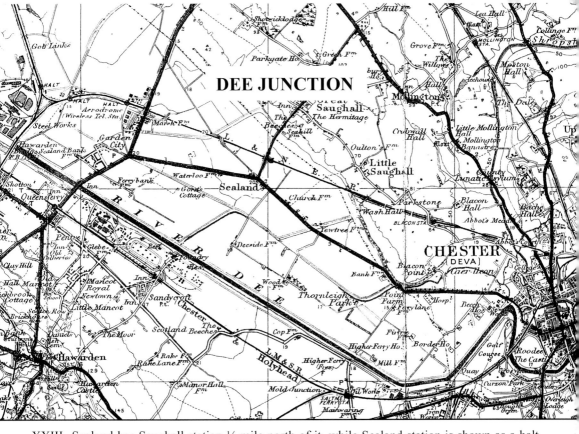

XXIII. Sealand has Saughall station ¼ mile north of it, while Sealand station is shown as a halt near the aerodrome and wireless telegraphy station. The map was published in 1919 and is scaled at 1ins to 1 mile. Dee Junction is the name for the triangular junction, from the top of which runs our route to Chester. The line to Chester closed to passengers in 1968 and will be visited first.

59.   No. 142043 runs south on 19th April 1986 and some of the British Steel sidings are visible. The works was operated by Corus Coated Products Division for many years. The box was erected in 1930 to a GCR design and had 65 levers, later reduced to 25. This was West Box originally and was still in use in 2013. (J.Whitehouse)

60.   The works is seen from the cab of no. 25275 on 14th July 1976, as it enters Shotwick sidings with iron ore from Bidston Dock. John Summer's family founded the steel works here in 1896 and specialised in galvanised steel. A century later, up to three trains daily were loaded with steel at 400°C in South Wales and delivered here. (T.Heavyside)

61.   No. 08802 is hauling empty timber wagons from Shotton Paper Company on 24th March 1999. Approximately two miles north of Dee Marsh Junction, Shotwick sidings were constructed to allow the ore trains from Bidston Dock to enter Shotton Steel Works site from the north. When the ore trains ceased running, the sidings were allowed to decay. Eventually they were used to serve Shotton Paper Mill. (D.E.Pool)

To Chester Northgate
SEALAND

62.   Welsh Road Halt opened on 17th June 1918 for public use and was renamed Sealand on 14th September 1931. It was closed on 9th September 1968, but was for forces personnel only in 1938-56 and is seen in 1951. The rods lead to a 20-lever box, which was in use until 14th September 1981. It was unusual in controlling a level crossing over an aircraft runway on Sealand Airfield. There were sliding gates in place from 1942 into the 1960s, plus two sidings for the RAF. (Stations UK)

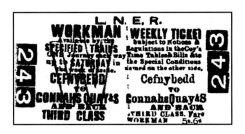

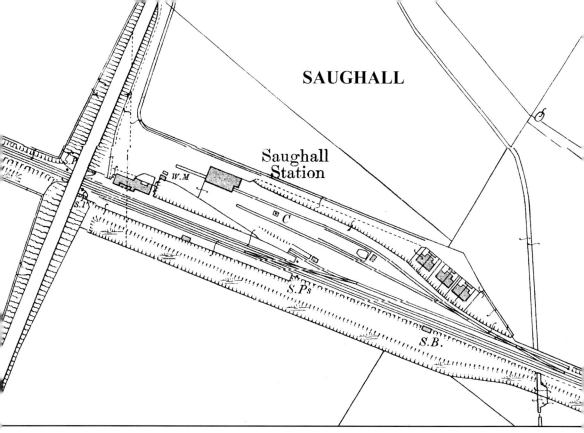

SAUGHALL

Saughall
Station

XXIV. The 1911 map has the signal box lower right. It had a 21-lever frame and was closed on 21st July 1957. The yard crane was rated at 5-tons.

63.   The fine details were recorded in about 1920 on a postcard. Two wires sufficed for communication. The village housed about 800 souls in 1901. When the remaining single line closed in 1992, the freight trains between Warrington and Dee Marsh had to run via Wrexham and reverse at Croes Newydd. (LOSA)

64.   This westward view is from about 1960. Both passenger and freight services were withdrawn from this rural station on 1st February 1954. The line was closed altogether in 1984, then reopened as a single track for freight. Following final closure in 1992, this section became a footpath/cycleway. The station was in Wales, but the village is in England. (LOSA)

BLACON

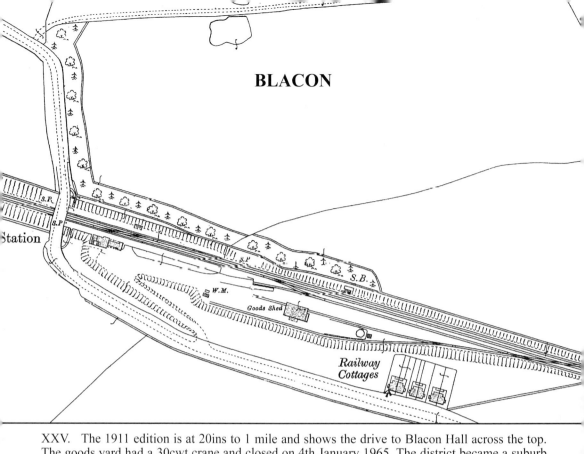

XXV. The 1911 edition is at 20ins to 1 mile and shows the drive to Blacon Hall across the top. The goods yard had a 30cwt crane and closed on 4th January 1965. The district became a suburb of Chester.

65. A panorama recorded on 6th June 1959 includes extensive housing and another dramatic station. "Wirral style" was the name applied by many railway observers. (R.M.Casserley)

66.　　Steps were provided from the road to both platforms to avoid the need for a footbridge. A DMU bound for Chester Northgate was recorded on 19th October 1963. The signal box is behind the camera. Its 21-lever frame was not used after 6th October 1963. (E.Wilmshurst)

L. N. E. R.
SERVICE MILITARY Etc.
FOR CONDITIONS SEE BACK
Available for three days, including day of issue
SEALAND to
WENDOVER
Via Chester G. W. Ry. & Aylesbury
THIRD / S.M. \ CLASS
WENDOVER
073　073

2nd - SINGLE　　SINGLE - 2nd
Sealand to
Sealand　　　　　Sealand
Blacon　　　　　Blacon
BLACON
(M)　1/2　Fare　1/2　(M)
For conditions see over　For conditions see over
5007　5007

CHESTER LIVERPOOL ROAD

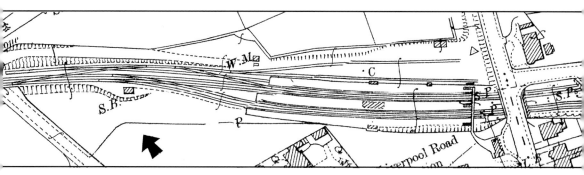

XXVI. The 1899 survey shows a single path from the station building leading to the footbridge.

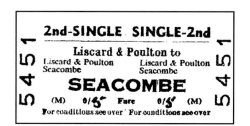

67.   The only information available for this photograph is that it was taken in 1921. The private owner wagons would be unloaded from the other side by local coal merchants. (Milepost 92½)

68.   A westward panorama from about 1930 includes the goods yard, which closed on 5th April 1951. Passenger service ceased on 3rd December 1951. In the distance is the 1890 signal box, which had 36 levers and closed on 14th June 1970. It was called Liverpool Road Junction. (Stations UK)

69.   A footbridge view in 1954 shows the tracks converging. Those on the left ceased to carry passengers to Chester in 1968, but the route on the right was used for freight until 1992. (Stations UK)

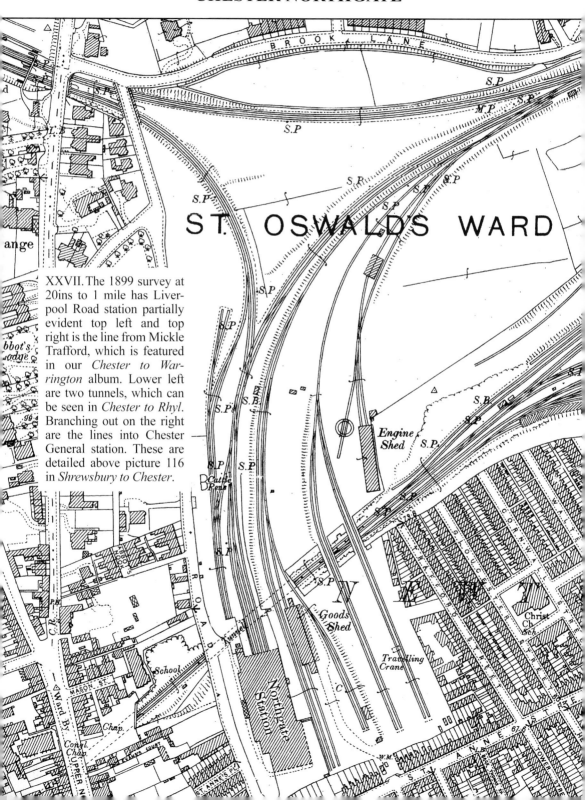

ST. OSWALD'S WARD

XXVII. The 1899 survey at 20ins to 1 mile has Liverpool Road station partially evident top left and top right is the line from Mickle Trafford, which is featured in our *Chester to Warrington* album. Lower left are two tunnels, which can be seen in *Chester to Rhyl*. Branching out on the right are the lines into Chester General station. These are detailed above picture 116 in *Shrewsbury to Chester*.

70.   The photographer is on Victoria Road bridge in 1921, as a freight train runs west along the top of the triangle. In the background is the massive water tank and the engine shed is on the right. (Milepost 92½)

71.   The prospective passenger's perspective is seen in about 1930, when gas lighting prevailed. The LNER then offered the best route to Manchester, using the former CLC route. The station had opened on 1st May 1875 for trains from that line. (Stations UK)

72.   With steam leaking from its injector, class C13 0-6-2T no. 5457 is being prepared to depart. The leading vehicle is a parcels van, fitted with a ducket from which the guard can observe the train when running. (LOSA)

73.   The complete roofing is evident as two 0-6-2Ts wait to leave. The two centre roads were used for carriage storage. Many such sidings had end loading facilities for the horse-drawn carriages of the gentry. (Milepost 92½)

74.　　The signals offered a choice of arrival platform and are seen on 9th May 1949, along with the coaling dock. Many were fitted with roofing during the blackout of World War II. In the distance is Chester South Box, which had 32 levers and was worked from 1889 until 6th October 1969, when the station closed. The locomotive is class C13 no. 67414. (LOSA)

75.　　Seen on the same day is class C13 no. 67429 and it is leaving for either Wrexham or Bidston. The massive goods shed is included. (LOSA)

76.   The acoustics would have been welcome for passengers arriving, but peace soon prevailed. The calm was recorded on 10th August 1953 as former CLC stock rested. (H.C.Casserley)

77.   The 2.30 departure for Wrexham Central is pictured on 19th September 1959, behind no. 82021. This was one of the class 3MT 2-6-2Ts introduced by BR in 1952. A DMU is at the other platform. (H.C.Casserley)

78.   The ex-CLC engine shed was photographed on 1st May 1960, with a DMU in residence. It closed that year, having housed 9 ex-GCR engines in 1950 and 11 BR ones in 1959. Its BR code was 6D. (R.S.Carpenter)

79.   On the left on 2nd July 1966 is a DMU bound for Manchester, while the one on the right is destined for Wrexham. A flat-pack shed was erected on the left, after the loss of that platform's roof. (J.M.Tolson/F.Hornby coll.)

80.   Seen not long before closure, the entrance was stark and unwelcoming. However, the goods shed was still standing. The Northgate Arena sports complex now occupies the area. (Milepost 92½)

BURTON POINT

XXVIII. The 1912 edition confirms the low population levels found near the 1896 route through the centre of the Wirral. This station did not open until 1st August 1899. It closed early, along with its goods yard, on 5th December 1955.

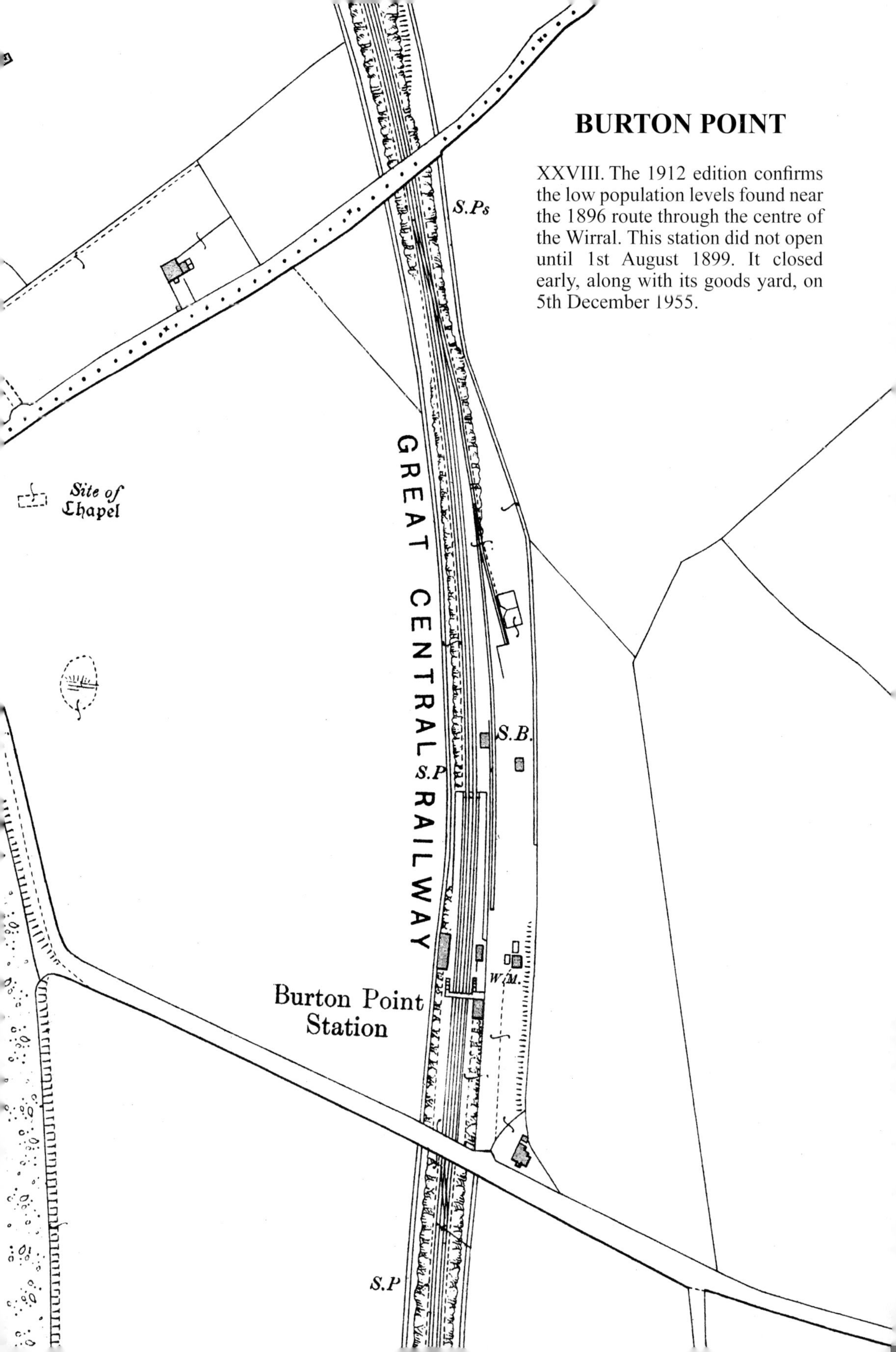

S.Ps

Site of Chapel

G R E A T   C E N T R A L   R A I L W A Y

S.P

S.B.

S.P

W.M.

Burton Point Station

S.P

81.   Shortage of staff meant that the track gang had to pose for the postcard photographer. The view is southwards, hence the dark faces. The signal box was behind the camera; its 22 lever frame was used between 1899 and 6th January 1962. (P.Laming coll.)

82.   The brickwork was basically yellow, with red courses at the extremities of the upper windows. This 1953 panorama shows repairs to the platform in progress. The entrance was at first floor level and passengers emerged from the booking hall onto the footbridge landing. The main building was still standing in 2012. (Stations UK)

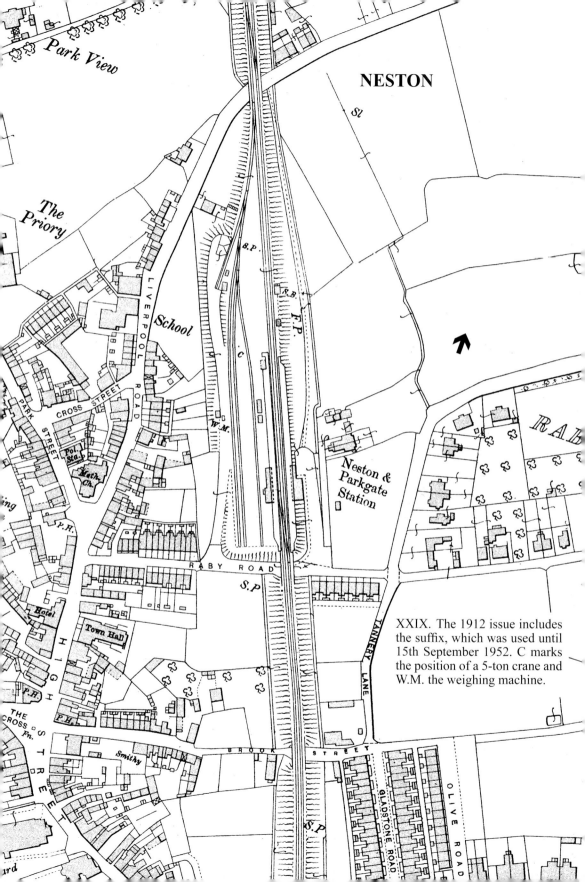

NESTON

Park View

The Priory

School

Liverpool Road

Cross Street

Park Street

High Street

Neston & Parkgate Station

Raby Road

Tannery Lane

RAB

Town Hall

Brook Street

Gladstone Road

Olive Road

Smithy

Hotel

Pol. Sta.

Meth. Ch.

P.H.

P.H.

The Cross

S.P.

S.P.

S.P.

S.P.

F.P.

W.M.

C

St

XXIX. The 1912 issue includes the suffix, which was used until 15th September 1952. C marks the position of a 5-ton crane and W.M. the weighing machine.

83.   The chimney is just visible on this GCR railmotor. The car is obstructing the view of the goods yard, which remained in use until 28th April 1969. Both platforms could take four cars in 2012. (LOSA)

84.   NESTON NORTH was the name in use from 15th September 1952 until 6th May 1968. The signal box is seen in 1946; it was also NESTON NORTH, but from 1st July 1950. Its 23-lever frame was taken out of use on 24th June 1969. The structure on the left is the water tank. (Stations UK)

85.   Its impressive exterior was photographed on 22nd April 1977. Its competitor had been Neston South, on the line from Hooton, but that had closed in 1956. (N.D.Mundy/R.M.Casserley coll.)

HESWALL

XXX. Another 1912 extract and this reveals extensive orchards nearby. The crane here was also rated at 5 tons. The suffix shown was used until 7th May 1973. The other Heswall station was close to the River Dee and near to, what is called today, Heswall Lower Village.

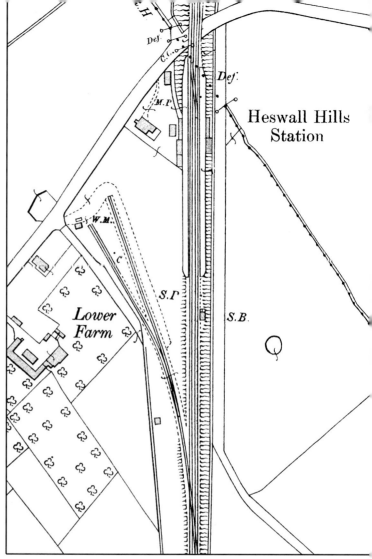

86. This 1946 panorama looking south features the girders of the road bridge and the sloping roofs over the stairs.
(Stations UK)

87.   The down pick-up goods is seen on 5th April 1957. The yard is much lower and was in use until 30th October 1965, when the station became unstaffed. The box had 20 levers and was manned until 5th January 1981. (H.B.Priestley)

88.   A Derby DMU is working from New Brighton to Wrexham Central on 20th September 1965. The buildings were still heated by coal and the platforms lit by oil. (R.S.Carpenter)

89.   The up platform appeared insecure when photographed on 26th June 2008, as all the fence posts had to be supported by scaffold poles. Both platforms then took three coaches. (V.Mitchell)

90.   The 11.32 Bidston to Wrexham Central was worked by no. 150262 on 24th October 2012. New fencing and smart shelters were on offer at this location by that time. (A.C.Hartless)

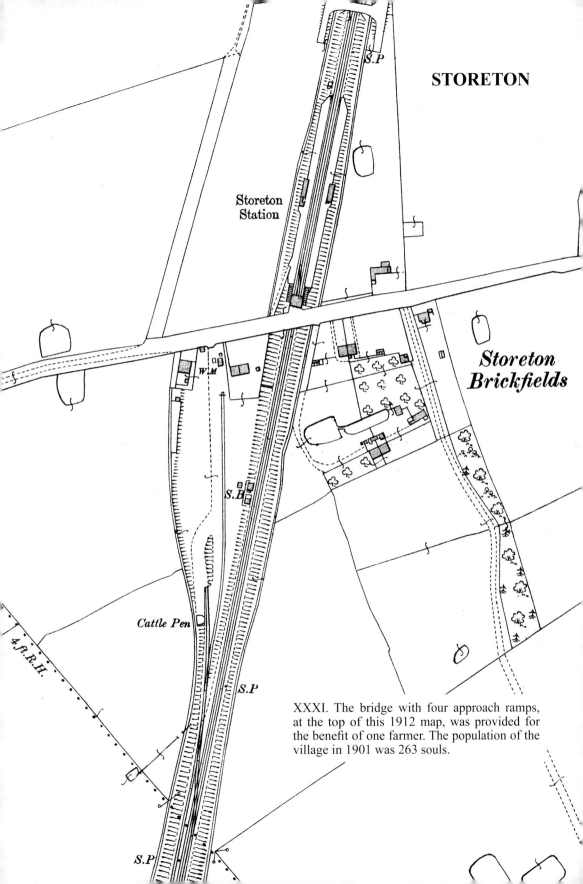

STORETON

Storeton
Station

S.P

*Storeton
Brickfields*

W.M

S.B

4 ft. R.H.

Cattle Pen

S.P

XXXI. The bridge with four approach ramps,
at the top of this 1912 map, was provided for
the benefit of one farmer. The population of the
village in 1901 was 263 souls.

S.P

91.　　This 1946 northward panorama is from the top of the steps leading to the down platform. The farm accommodation bridge is in the distance, while on the right is a screen to hide the door to the gents. (Stations UK)

92.　　A view from just prior to closure on 3rd December 1951 includes more trouble with fencing. The steps from the booking hall are on the right. The goods yard was beyond the bridge and it closed on 3rd February 1964. The nearby signal box had 23 levers and lasted until 2nd July 1965. (R.S.Carpenter coll.)

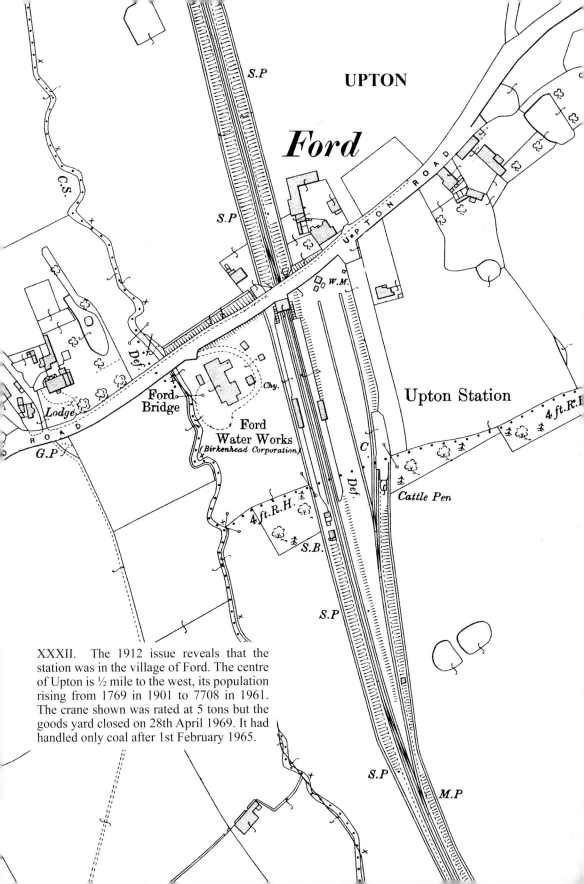

UPTON

Ford

S.P

C.S.

Def.

Ford
Bridge

Lodge

ROAD

G.P

S.P

S.P

W.M.

Chy.

Ford
Water Works
(Birkenhead Corporation)

4 ft.R.H.

S.B.

S.P

Upton Station

4 ft.R.

C

Def.

Cattle Pen

S.P

M.P

XXXII. The 1912 issue reveals that the station was in the village of Ford. The centre of Upton is ½ mile to the west, its population rising from 1769 in 1901 to 7708 in 1961. The crane shown was rated at 5 tons but the goods yard closed on 28th April 1969. It had handled only coal after 1st February 1965.

93.   This northward view was the subject of a postcard, but locomotive details were not included. The booking hall on a bridge was a concept widely practised by the GCR. (P.Laming coll.)

94.   A signal box was an unusual subject to include on a postcard, but interest was added by the presence of a lady and a waterworks chimney. The 24-lever frame was in use until 25th June 1969. (P.Laming coll.)

95. A rare close view of an elevated station includes oil lighting, but no plumbing details. Staffing ceased on 20th April 1969. The crossover lasted until the goods yard closed. (LOSA)

96. The building was demolished and the steps were replaced by long ramps. The 12.54 Wrexham Central to Bidston was worked by no. 142047 on 23rd October 1986. The platforms were later surfaced for four cars only. (T.Heavyside)

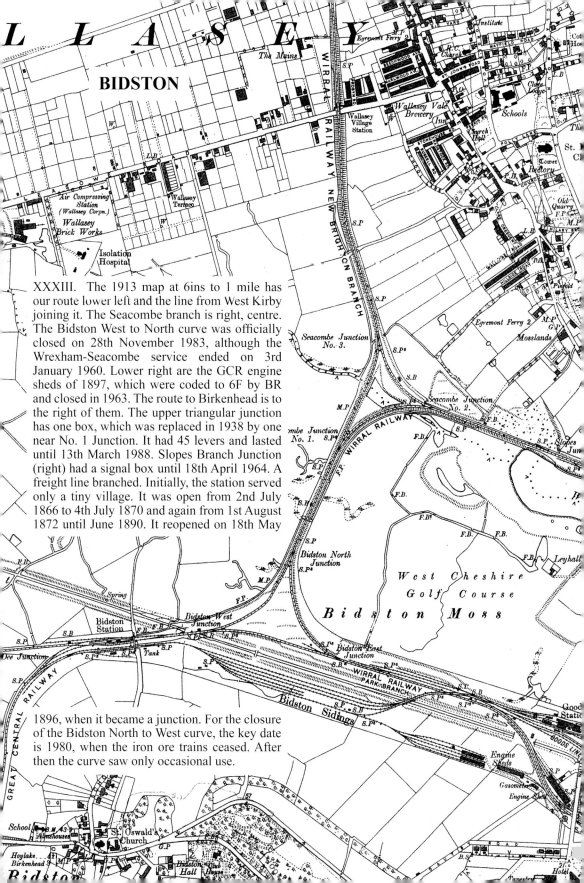

XXXIII. The 1913 map at 6ins to 1 mile has our route lower left and the line from West Kirby joining it. The Seacombe branch is right, centre. The Bidston West to North curve was officially closed on 28th November 1983, although the Wrexham-Seacombe service ended on 3rd January 1960. Lower right are the GCR engine sheds of 1897, which were coded to 6F by BR and closed in 1963. The route to Birkenhead is to the right of them. The upper triangular junction has one box, which was replaced in 1938 by one near No. 1 Junction. It had 45 levers and lasted until 13th March 1988. Slopes Branch Junction (right) had a signal box until 18th April 1964. A freight line branched. Initially, the station served only a tiny village. It was open from 2nd July 1866 to 4th July 1870 and again from 1st August 1872 until June 1890. It reopened on 18th May

1896, when it became a junction. For the closure of the Bidston North to West curve, the key date is 1980, when the iron ore trains ceased. After then the curve saw only occasional use.

97. A 1939 panorama from the footbridge has the West Kirby lines disappearing into the mist and on the left are the goods lines curving to join the route south to Shotton. The station is at its optimum; third rail electrification had been introduced in 1938. The LMS East Box of 1937 had 45 levers and also lasted until 1994. (Stations UK)

98. A similar view on 17th October 1953 features class 04 2-8-0 no. 63742 and class J39 0-6-0 no. 64742 approaching the crossing. On the right is Bidston Dee Junction Box of 1938. It had 65 levers and closed on 18th September 1994. It had taken over the work of Bidston West Junction Box in 1938; this box had worked North Junction as well. (N.Sprinks)

99.   Fresh paint is evident widely on the well lit station on 19th September 1959, by which time much of the marshland was used for golf. No. 82020 is a BR class 3MT 2-6-2T, a type built from 1952 onwards. (H.C.Casserley)

100.   The locomotive shed and sidings were photographed on 2nd July 1961. The code was 6F and there were eight engines allocated here in 1950, the figure rising to 14 in 1959. Closure came on 11th February 1963 and goods traffic ceased on 29th July 1968. (R.S.Carpenter)

101. The footbridge viewpoint can be enjoyed on 16th July 1976, as no. M29273 runs in from Liverpool, bound for West Kirby. Waiting on the curve is a train of iron ore loaded in the docks in the background and destined for the steel works at Shotton. Steam traction had been used until 6th November 1967. (T.Heavyside)

102. The skyline had been changed by the coming of the M53. It is 1st April 1978 and no. 25294 is heading the "Hundred of Wirral" tour and is turning onto the New Brighton line. The curve closed in 1983. Since 1978, DMUs have terminated here, while EMUs provide the connections. Dwell time for the Wrexham trains before reversal was often quite short, as the electric route was being obstructed. They could use either platform face. Both could take six cars. (T.Heavyside)

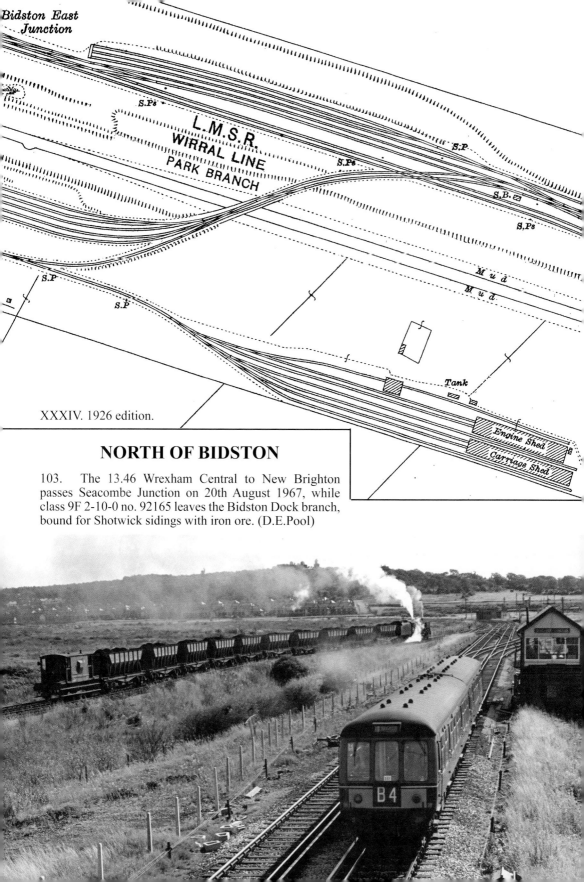

Bidston East Junction

S.Ps

L.M.S.R. WIRRAL LINE PARK BRANCH

S.P

S.Ps

S.B.

S.Ps

S.P

S.P

Mud

Mud

Tank

Engine Shed

Carriage Shed

XXXIV. 1926 edition.

NORTH OF BIDSTON

103.   The 13.46 Wrexham Central to New Brighton passes Seacombe Junction on 20th August 1967, while class 9F 2-10-0 no. 92165 leaves the Bidston Dock branch, bound for Shotwick sidings with iron ore. (D.E.Pool)

Seacombe Branch
LISCARD & POULTON

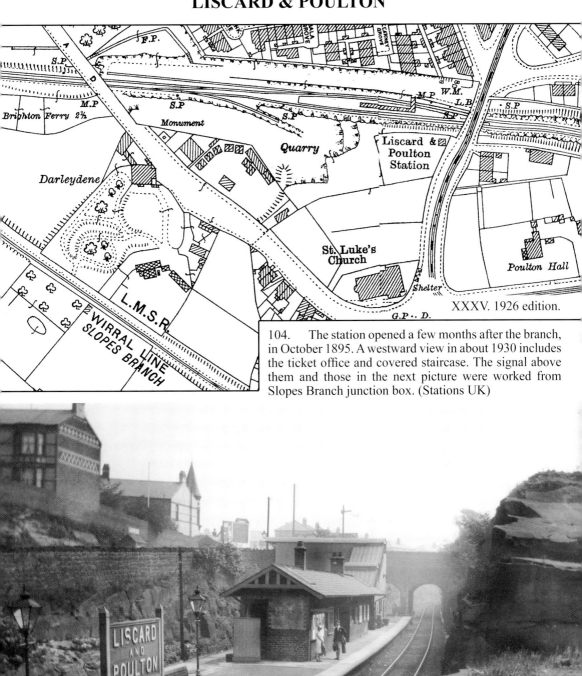

XXXV. 1926 edition.

104. The station opened a few months after the branch, in October 1895. A westward view in about 1930 includes the ticket office and covered staircase. The signal above them and those in the next picture were worked from Slopes Branch junction box. (Stations UK)

105. The goods yard was recorded in August 1953 and it was in use until 5th December 1960. It had a 5-ton crane at one period. The sandstone cutting has now partially vanished, the trackbed being used for a link road to the M53. (Stations UK)

SEACOMBE

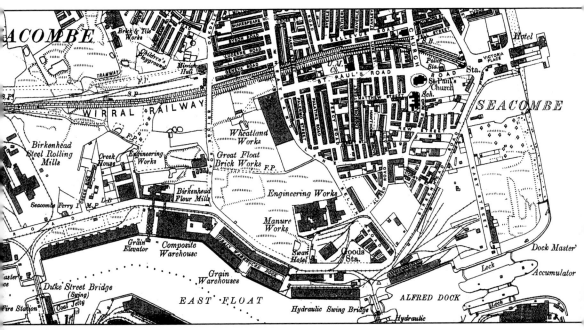

XXXVI. The 1906 edition at 6ins to 1 mile reveals that the station was close to the seafront, a popular destination. The branch had received trains from New Brighton until 1911, from West Kirby until 1938 and from Wrexham until 1960.

106.   Church Road and the signal box are in the background. The latter closed on 18th April 1964, as did Goods Yard Box. Ex-GCR class C13 4-4-2T no. 67428 is about to run round its train from Wrexham Central on 26th June 1954. (N.Sprinks)

107.   The locomotive has completed its run round and we gain a closer look at its train before returning to Wrexham. The station had the suffix "& Egremont" between July 1901 and January 1953. The clock tower is on the ferry terminal. (N.Sprinks)

108.   The end of the line was recorded long after the last passenger had left on 4th January 1960. The goods yard continued in use until the end of that year. (Bentley coll.)

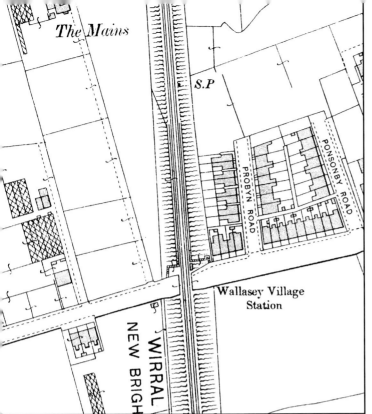

WALLASEY VILLAGE

XXXVII. We return to the New Brighton branch of the Wirral Railway, which opened on 30th March 1888. However, this station did not come into use until March 1907. The 1910 edition shows that some residential development had taken place, but that glasshouses were numerous. They are shown with diamonds.

109. We look north in 1960. Electrification was achieved in 1938, with through services from New Brighton to Liverpool. Residents had been frustrated as the Mersey Railway had provided electric trains under the river since 1903. (Stations UK)

110. A Liverpool to New Brighton EMU arrives on 28th July 1979. The steps to the down platform are on the left. The station had been rebuilt in concrete just prior to electrification. (T.Heavyside)

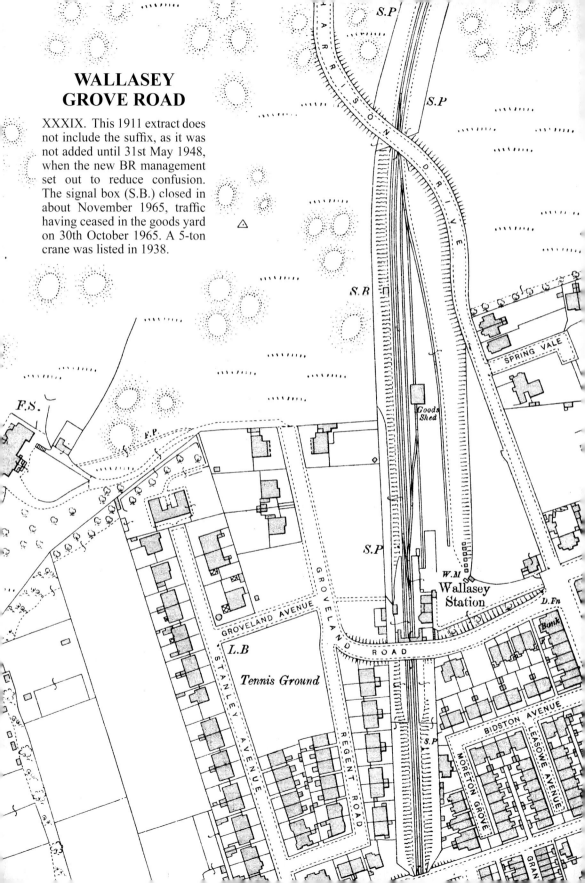

WALLASEY
GROVE ROAD

XXXIX. This 1911 extract does not include the suffix, as it was not added until 31st May 1948, when the new BR management set out to reduce confusion. The signal box (S.B.) closed in about November 1965, traffic having ceased in the goods yard on 30th October 1965. A 5-ton crane was listed in 1938.

Goods Shed

S.P

S.R

S.P

SPRING VALE

S.P

F.S.

F.P.

GROVELAND AVENUE

STANLEY AVENUE

L.B

Tennis Ground

GROVELAND ROAD

REGENT ROAD

W.M
Wallasey Station

D. Fn

Bank

S.P

BIDSTON AVENUE

MORETON GROVE

EASOWE AVENUE

GRAN

111.   The station was the temporary terminus of the branch from 2nd January to 30th March of 1888. The WR features are notable, particularly the name on the canopy, in this view from around 1910. (Stations UK)

112.   A southward panorama in 1950 includes an LMS Hawkseye sign below the canopy and an electrified crossover, which was seldom used. The covered footbridge is adjacent to Groveland Road bridge. (Stations UK)

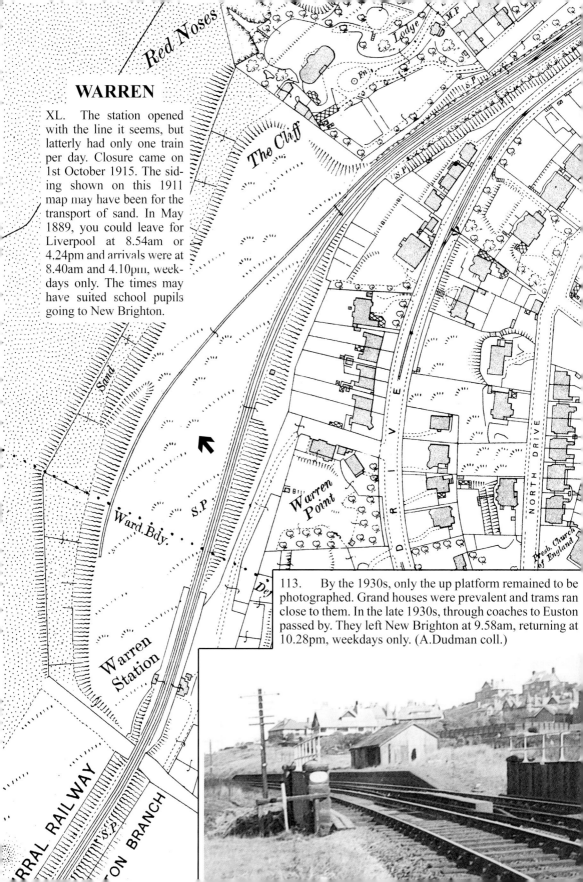

WARREN

XL. The station opened with the line it seems, but latterly had only one train per day. Closure came on 1st October 1915. The siding shown on this 1911 map may have been for the transport of sand. In May 1889, you could leave for Liverpool at 8.54am or 4.24pm and arrivals were at 8.40am and 4.10pm, weekdays only. The times may have suited school pupils going to New Brighton.

113. By the 1930s, only the up platform remained to be photographed. Grand houses were prevalent and trams ran close to them. In the late 1930s, through coaches to Euston passed by. They left New Brighton at 9.58am, returning at 10.28pm, weekdays only. (A.Dudman coll.)

NEW BRIGHTON

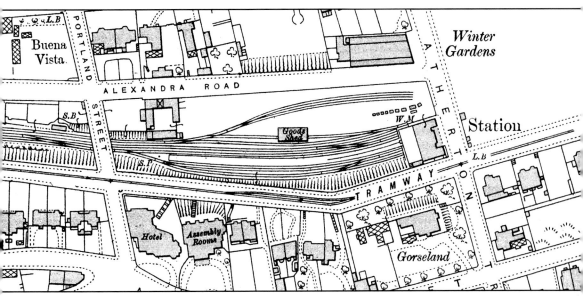

XLI. The 1911 edition presents spacious dwellings many with impressive drives. The Birkenhead Corporation Tramway ran from 1901 to 1937 and successfully reduced railway passenger numbers, both here and at Seacombe.

114.   The railway again used the canopy for words, but must have had visitors with myopic vision. The entrance was infinitely more impressive than that at Seacombe. (Stations U.K.)

115.   Hopefully, most passengers arrived in dry weather as the train stopped in the position shown to enable the locomotive to use the crossover. It would later propel the empty train towards the buffers. (P.Laming coll.)

116.   Visible is much of the goods yard, which closed on 30th October 1965. The panorama was recorded from Portland Street in the Edwardian era. Included is the spire of St. James' Church and the New Brighton Tower of 1900. It consumed more than 1000 tons of steel and was the tallest structure in Britain at 567ft. It was dismantled in 1919-21, due to wartime neglect. (P.Laming coll.)

117.   A 1950 photograph includes the goods shed, but not the 5-ton crane. The platform canopy arrived belatedly, in about 1938 and was of concrete construction. Behind the Hawkseye sign is an ex-MR EMU. (Stations UK)

118. All sidings were eventually electrified for stock berthing. The lighting had moved from mantles to bulbs to tubes in three photographs. (D.K.Jones)

→ 119. All five roads were occupied on 13th April 1985. Centre is EMU no. 28394 on a tour run by the LCGB called the "Class 503 Farewell". It covered most of the electric network for £8.50. (D.E.Pool)

→ 120. The final link with the past was lost on 18th September 1994, when the semaphore signals were taken out of use, along with the 44-lever signal box, just visible beyond the bridge. By that time, all platforms on the branch were designated for six coaches and had a steady traffic. (J.Whitehouse)

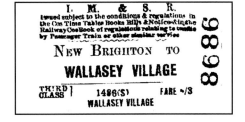

MP Middleton Press
EVOLVING THE ULTIMATE RAIL ENCYCLOPEDIA

Easebourne Lane, Midhurst, West Sussex.
GU29 9AZ   Tel:01730 813169

www.middletonpress.co.uk   email:info@middletonpress.co.uk
A-978 0 906520   B- 978 1 873793   C- 978 1 901706   D-978 1 904474
E - 978 1 906008   F - 978 1 908174

All titles listed below were in print at time of publication - please check current availability by looking at our website - **www.middletonpress.co.uk** or by requesting a Brochure which includes our *LATEST* RAILWAY TITLES also our TRAMWAY, TROLLEYBUS, MILITARY and COASTAL series